SCOTT FORESMAN · ADDISON WESLEY

Mathematics

Grade 2

Enrichment Masters/Workbook

Editorial Offices: Glenview, Illinois • Parsippany, New Jersey • New York, New York

Sales Offices: Parsippany, New Jersey • Duluth, Georgia • Glenview, Illinois
Coppell, Texas • Ontario, California • Mesa, Arizona

Overview

Enrichment Masters/Workbook enhances student learning by actively involving students in different areas of mathematical reasoning. Activities often involve students in real-world situations, some of which may have more than one right answer. Thus, the masters motivate students to find alternate solutions to a given problem.

How to use

The *Enrichment Masters/Workbook* is designed so that the teacher can use it in many different ways.

- As a teaching tool to guide students in exploring a specific type of thinking skill. Making a transparency of the worksheet provides an excellent way to expedite this process as students work at their desks along with the teacher.

- As an enrichment worksheet that challenges and motivates students to hone their thinking skills.

- As independent or group work.

- As a homework assignment that encourages students to involve their parents in the educational process.

ISBN 0-328-04933-6

2 3 4 5 6 7 8 9 10 V084 09 08 07 06 05 04 03

Table of Contents

Table of Contents continued

Balloon Party

Write the numbers to show how many there are in all.
Use each number in a balloon only once.
You may use counters if you need to.

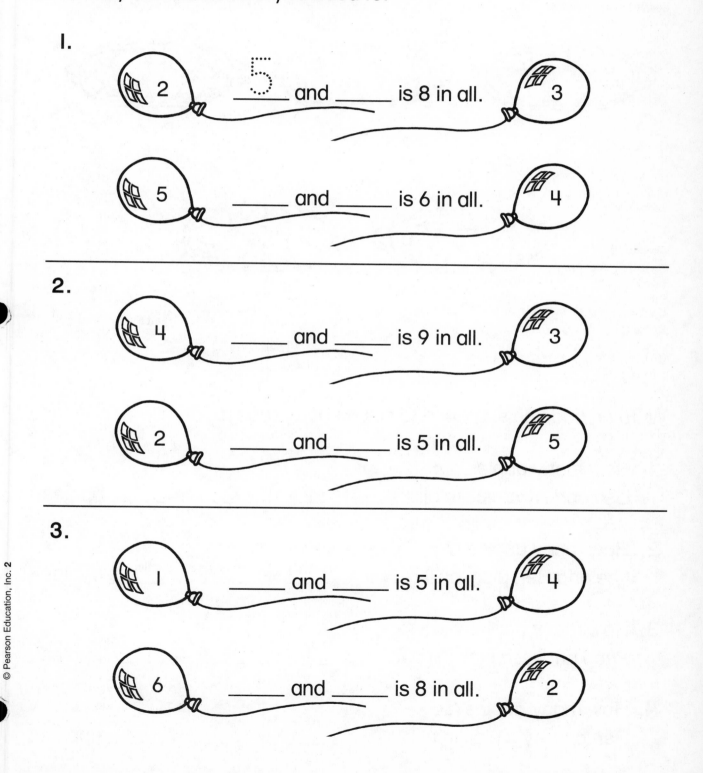

1.

2 _____ 5 ____ and _____ is 8 in all. 3

5 _____ and _____ is 6 in all. 4

2.

4 _____ and _____ is 9 in all. 3

2 _____ and _____ is 5 in all. 5

3.

1 _____ and _____ is 5 in all. 4

6 _____ and _____ is 8 in all. 2

Name _____

Apple Picking

Five friends went apple picking.

Lisa   Lee   Paco

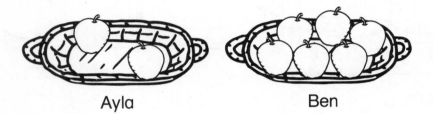

Ayla   Ben

Write an addition sentence to solve each problem.

1. How many apples did
   Lisa and Ayla pick in all?   5 + _____ = _____ apples

2. How many apples did
   Lee and Ben pick in all?   _____ + _____ = _____ apples

3. How many apples did
   Paco and Lisa pick in all?   _____ + _____ = _____ apples

4. How many apples did
   Ben and Ayla pick in all?   _____ + _____ = _____ apples

Time for Lunch

The table shows how many children ordered
school lunches for one week.

School Lunches Ordered

	Monday	Tuesday	Wednesday	Thursday	Friday
Grade 1	2	3	4	6	3
Grade 2	5	4	7	1	8

Write a number sentence to solve each problem.

1. How many lunches did Grade 1 order on Monday? ___2___

   How many lunches did Grade 2 order on Monday? _____

   How many lunches were
   ordered in all on Monday? _____ lunches

2. How many lunches did Grade 1 order on Friday? _____

   How many lunches did Grade 2 order on Friday? _____

   How many lunches were
   ordered altogether on Friday? _____ lunches

3. How many lunches did Grade 2 order on Thursday? _____

   How many lunches did Grade 2 order on Friday? _____

   How many lunches were ordered
   in Grade 2 on these two days? _____ lunches

Name _____

Making Fruit Salad

Help Carla make fruit salad.
Decide how many pieces of each fruit you will use.
Cross out the pieces of fruit you do not use.
Write the numbers.

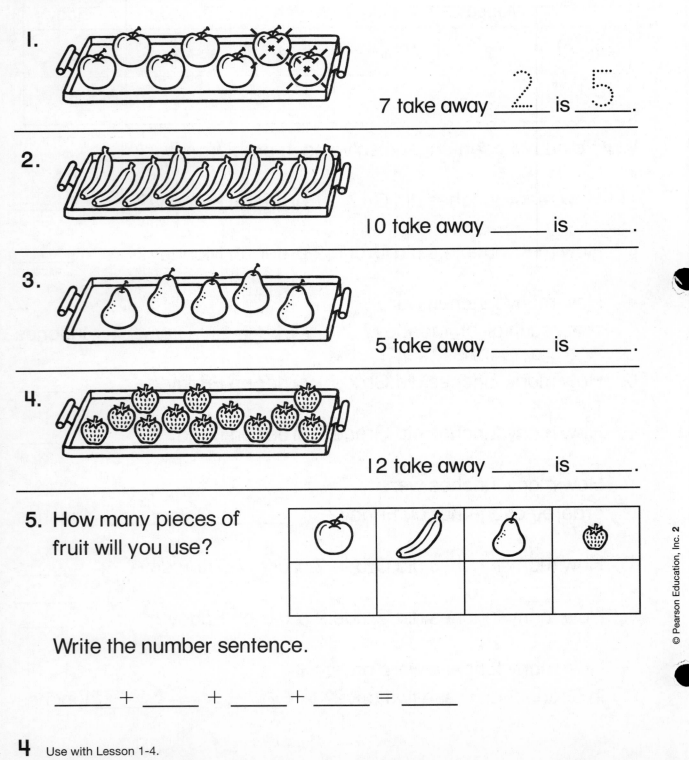

1.

7 take away __2__ is __5__.

2.

10 take away _____ is _____.

3.

5 take away _____ is _____.

4.

12 take away _____ is _____.

5. How many pieces of
fruit will you use?

Write the number sentence.

_____ + _____ + _____ + _____ = _____

Name _____

Counting Birds

Mrs. Johnson's class went bird watching.
The graph shows the birds they saw.

Birds We Saw

One 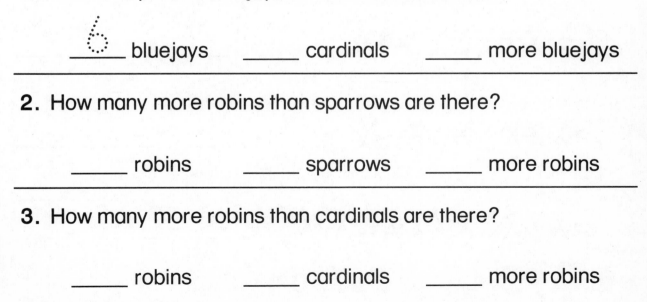 stands for 1 bird.

Use the graph to solve each problem.

1. How many more bluejays than cardinals are there?

   _6_ bluejays   _____ cardinals   _____ more bluejays

2. How many more robins than sparrows are there?

   _____ robins   _____ sparrows   _____ more robins

3. How many more robins than cardinals are there?

   _____ robins   _____ cardinals   _____ more robins

Disappearing Beads

Look at the crossed out beads.
Write a subtraction sentence.

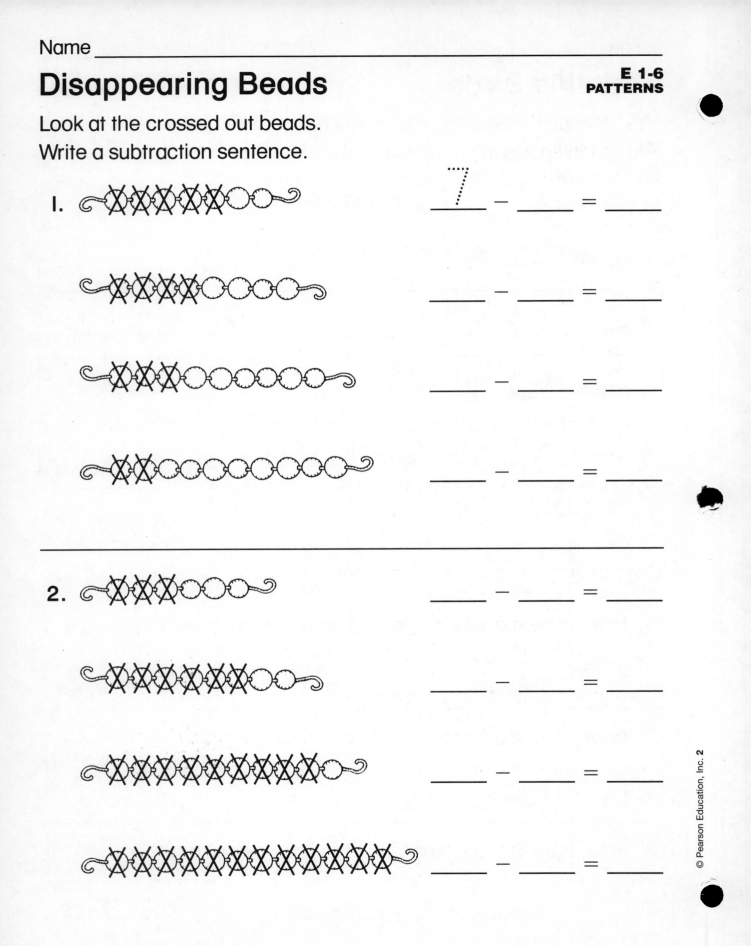

1.

____7____ – _____ = _____

_____ – _____ = _____

_____ – _____ = _____

_____ – _____ = _____

2.

_____ – _____ = _____

_____ – _____ = _____

_____ – _____ = _____

_____ – _____ = _____

© Pearson Education, Inc. 2

Obey the Rules

Decide if you need to add to or subtract from the number in the **In** column to get the number in the **Out** column. Then circle one of the rules to the right of the chart.

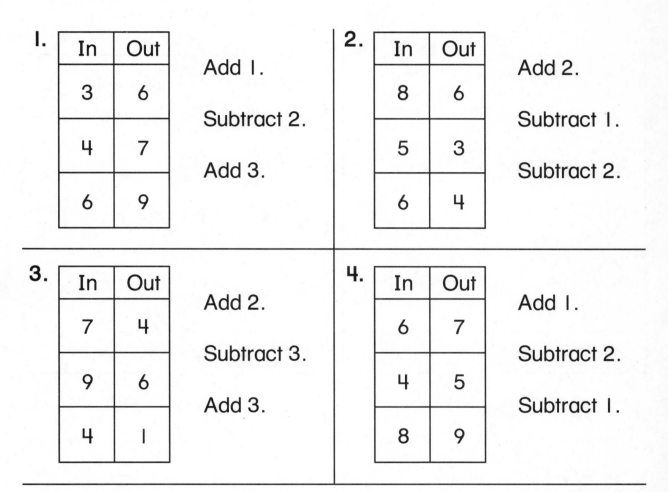

1.

In	Out
3	6
4	7
6	9

Add 1.

Subtract 2.

Add 3.

2.

In	Out
8	6
5	3
6	4

Add 2.

Subtract 1.

Subtract 2.

3.

In	Out
7	4
9	6
4	1

Add 2.

Subtract 3.

Add 3.

4.

In	Out
6	7
4	5
8	9

Add 1.

Subtract 2.

Subtract 1.

Write the rule.

5.

In	5	9	10
Out	4	8	9

The rule is _____.

Name _____

Picture Match Up

Find the group of pictures in Box 1 and
Box 2 that have the same objects.
Write two addition sentences to show
how many there are in all.

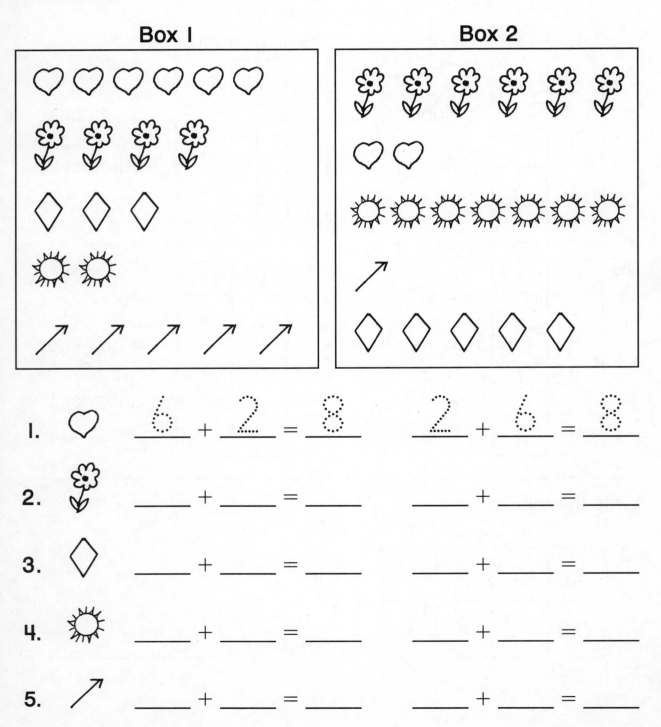

Box 1   **Box 2**

1. ♡   __6__ + __2__ = __8__   __2__ + __6__ = __8__

2. ❀   ____ + ____ = ____   ____ + ____ = ____

3. ◇   ____ + ____ = ____   ____ + ____ = ____

4. ☼   ____ + ____ = ____   ____ + ____ = ____

5. ↗   ____ + ____ = ____   ____ + ____ = ____

Finding 10

1. Find different ways to make 10.
Complete each number sentence.

$0 +$ __10__ $= 10$

_____ $+ 9 = 10$

$2 +$ _____ $= 10$

_____ $+ 7 = 10$

$4 +$ _____ $= 10$

_____ $+ 5 = 10$

2. Ring the pairs of numbers that make 10.
Use the number sentences above to help you.

4	2	3	5	5
1	6	6	3	1
9	3	2	8	0
0	7	1	7	10
9	6	5	8	5

Name _____

Lucky Facts

Draw the missing dots.
Write a fact family for each.

What's Missing?

Each problem has a missing part.
Fill in the missing numbers. Use counters or
draw pictures to help.

1. Beth has 4 pencils.

Aman has _____ pencils.

They have 10 pencils in all.

$4 +$ _____ $= 10$

2. Maura has 2 crayons.

Carlos has _____ crayons.

They have 11 crayons in all.

$2 +$ _____ $= 11$

3. Jiro has 7 books.

Deb has _____ books.

They have 12 books in all.

$7 +$ _____ $= 12$

4. Liz has 5 notebooks.

Paco has _____ notebooks.

They have 13 notebooks in all.

$5 +$ _____ $= 13$

5. Jarek has 1 paint can.

Patty has _____ paint cans.

They have 8 paint cans in all.

$1 +$ _____ $= 8$

6. Write your own problem.

_____

_____

_____

_____ $+$ _____ $=$ _____

Name _____

Find the Secret Number

Read the clues to find the secret number.

1.

```
7    6    7    8
12   9    3    5
```

I am inside the path.
I am the sum of 2 other numbers inside the path.

What number am I? _____

2.

```
10                    8
    6        13
         5
   11        9
3                   7
```

I am outside the path.
I am the difference of 2 numbers inside the path.
I am less than 5.

What number am I? _____

3.

```
        10
12              11
    5       8
  4     7     9
```

I am inside the path.
I am the sum of 2 other numbers inside the path.

What number am I? _____

4.

```
6
        9
  3
             8
   10              6
        4
              10
```

I am outside the path.
I am the difference of 2 other numbers outside the path.
I am greater than 5.

What number am I? _____

It's a Date

Karen starts school on September 7th.

September						
S	**M**	**T**	**W**	**T**	**F**	**S**
			1	2	3	
4	5	6	⑦	8	9	10
11	12	13	14	15	16	17
18	19	20	21	22	23	24
25	26	27	28	29	30	

Use the calendar to answer the questions.

1. Three days after school starts, Karen goes to soccer practice.

   What date will that be? _____

2. Two days after soccer practice, Karen goes to her friend's house.

   What date will that be? _____

3. Three days after Karen visits her friend, she goes to music lessons.

   What date will that be? _____

4. One day after music lessons, Karen goes to the movies.

   What date will that be? _____

Double Up

Solve the problem. Then write the addition fact.

1. Jacob wants to put the same number of
apples on each platter. He has 8 apples.
Draw the apples Jacob will put on each platter.

____ + ____ = ____

2. Luz wants to put the same number of
flowers in each flower box. She has 12 flowers.
Draw the flowers Luz will put in each box.

____ + ____ = ____

3. Elena wants to put the same number of
cups on each table. She has 10 cups.
Draw the cups Elena will put on each table.

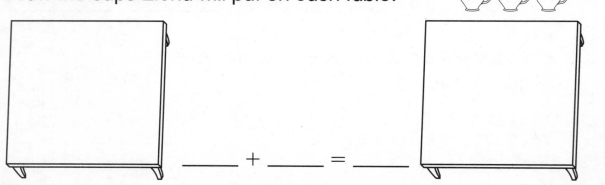

____ + ____ = ____

Number Riddles

Write an addition sentence to solve the problem.
Use doubles facts to help you.

1. 7 plus a number equals 13.
What is the number?

$7 + \underline{6} = 13$

The number is $\underline{6}$.

2. A number plus 9 equals 17.
What is the number?

$\underline{8} + \underline{9} = \underline{17}$

The number is $\underline{8}$.

3. 5 plus a number equals 11.
What is the number?

$\underline{} + \underline{} = \underline{}$

The number is _____.

4. A number plus 8 equals 16.
What is the number?

$\underline{} + \underline{} = \underline{}$

The number is _____.

5. A number plus 5 equals 9.
What is the number?

$\underline{} + \underline{} = \underline{}$

The number is _____.

6. 8 plus a number equals 15.
What is the number?

$\underline{} + \underline{} = \underline{}$

The number is _____.

7. A number plus 6 equals 12.
What is the number?

$\underline{} + \underline{} = \underline{}$

The number is _____.

8. A number plus 9 equals 19.
What is the number?

$\underline{} + \underline{} = \underline{}$

The number is _____.

Which Strategy?

Show 2 steps to solve each problem.
Circle the strategy you used in Step 1.

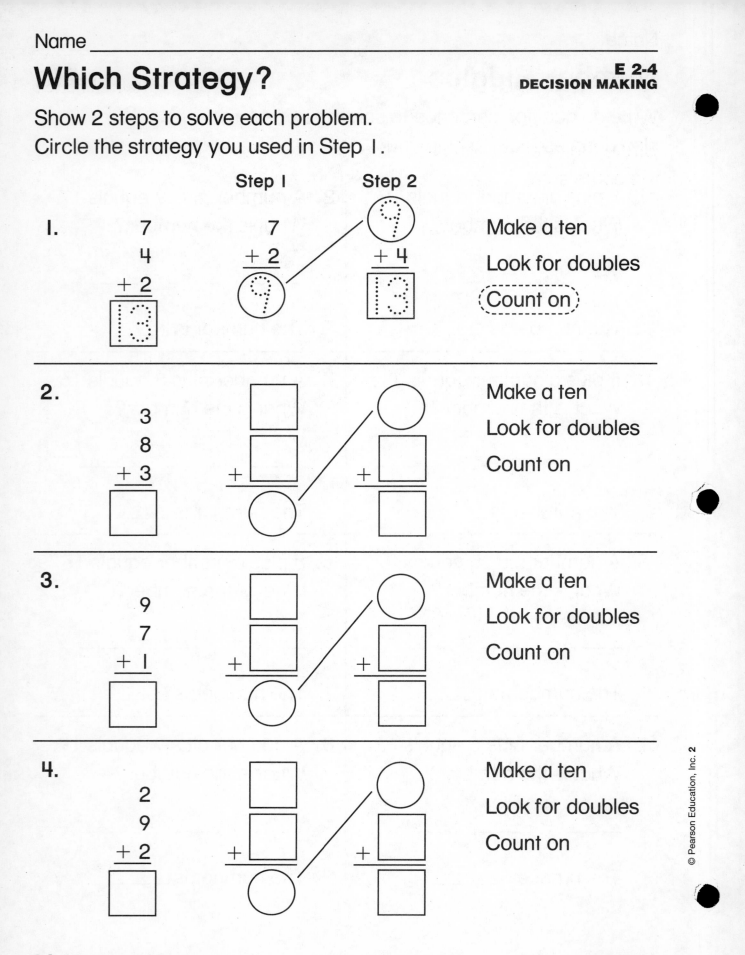

	Step 1	Step 2	

1.
$$\begin{array}{r} 7 \\ 4 \\ + 2 \\ \hline 13 \end{array}$$

Make a ten
Look for doubles
(Count on)

2.
$$\begin{array}{r} 3 \\ 8 \\ + 3 \\ \hline \end{array}$$

Make a ten
Look for doubles
Count on

3.
$$\begin{array}{r} 9 \\ 7 \\ + 1 \\ \hline \end{array}$$

Make a ten
Look for doubles
Count on

4.
$$\begin{array}{r} 2 \\ 9 \\ + 2 \\ \hline \end{array}$$

Make a ten
Look for doubles
Count on

Match a Sum

Add.

Circle the addition problem that has the same sum.

1. $9 + 6 =$ _____

$$\begin{array}{r} 10 \\ +\ 4 \\ \hline \end{array} \qquad \begin{array}{r} 10 \\ +\ 9 \\ \hline \end{array} \qquad \begin{array}{r} 10 \\ +\ 8 \\ \hline \end{array} \qquad \begin{array}{r} 10 \\ +\ 5 \\ \hline \end{array} \qquad \begin{array}{r} 10 \\ +\ 6 \\ \hline \end{array}$$

2. $9 + 8 =$ _____

$$\begin{array}{r} 10 \\ +\ 5 \\ \hline \end{array} \qquad \begin{array}{r} 10 \\ +\ 7 \\ \hline \end{array} \qquad \begin{array}{r} 10 \\ +\ 4 \\ \hline \end{array} \qquad \begin{array}{r} 10 \\ +\ 9 \\ \hline \end{array} \qquad \begin{array}{r} 10 \\ +\ 8 \\ \hline \end{array}$$

3. $9 + 5 =$ _____

$$\begin{array}{r} 10 \\ +\ 3 \\ \hline \end{array} \qquad \begin{array}{r} 10 \\ +\ 6 \\ \hline \end{array} \qquad \begin{array}{r} 10 \\ +\ 5 \\ \hline \end{array} \qquad \begin{array}{r} 10 \\ +\ 4 \\ \hline \end{array} \qquad \begin{array}{r} 10 \\ +\ 8 \\ \hline \end{array}$$

4. $9 + 7 =$ _____

$$\begin{array}{r} 10 \\ +\ 6 \\ \hline \end{array} \qquad \begin{array}{r} 10 \\ +\ 5 \\ \hline \end{array} \qquad \begin{array}{r} 10 \\ +\ 7 \\ \hline \end{array} \qquad \begin{array}{r} 10 \\ +\ 9 \\ \hline \end{array} \qquad \begin{array}{r} 10 \\ +\ 3 \\ \hline \end{array}$$

Money Exchange

Solve. Use dimes and pennies if you need to.

1. Mary has 8 pennies.
   Jay has 6 pennies.
   They exchange some pennies for 1 dime.
   How many pennies do they still have?

   1 dime and _____ pennies

---

2. Nancy has 7 pennies.
   Ahmed has 5 pennies.
   They exchange some pennies for 1 dime.
   How many pennies do they still have?

   1 dime and _____ pennies

---

3. Freddie has 4 pennies.
   Margie has 8 pennies.
   They exchange some pennies for 1 dime.
   How many pennies do they still have?

   1 dime and _____ pennies

---

4. Suki has 9 pennies.
   Marco has 7 pennies.
   They exchange some pennies for 1 dime.
   How many pennies do they still have?

   1 dime and _____ pennies

Clean-Up Day

The chart shows how many cans each child collected.

Cans Collected

Billy	Shayla	Lucky	Mia	Sharon	Yoshi
8	5	3	7	6	4

Use the data from the chart to fill in the blanks. Write an addition sentence to find the number of cans the students collected.

1. Billy collected __8__ cans. Lucky collected __3__ cans.

   __Yoshi__ collected 4 cans.

   How many cans did they collect in all?

   __8__ + __3__ + __4__ = __15__ cans

2. Shayla collected _____ cans. Lucky collected _____ cans.

   _____ collected 7 cans.
   How many cans did they collect in all?

   _____ + _____ + _____ = _____ cans

3. Mia collected _____ cans. Shayla collected _____ cans.

   _____ collected 3 cans.
   How many cans did they collect in all?

   _____ + _____ + _____ = _____ cans

Name _____

Sorry, Wrong Number

Find the pattern in each row.
One number is incorrect.
Cross it out and write the number
that continues the pattern.

1. 10   9   8   7   ~~5~~   5   4   3   ___6___

2. 3   2   3   2   3   2   1   2   ___

3. 14   12   10   8   7   4   2   0   ___

4. 9   8   9   8   9   8   9   7   ___

5. 18   17   16   15   16   13   12   11   ___

6. 21   19   17   15   12   11   9   7   ___

7. Make your own pattern with one number
    that does not fit. Ask a friend to solve it.

    ___ ___ ___ ___ ___ ___ ___ ___

Name _____

Sharing

Separate the objects into 2 equal groups.
Write a subtraction sentence and the related doubles fact.

1. Becky has 10 apples.
   She shares 5 apples with Tom.
   How many apples do they
   each have?

   What doubles fact helps you?

   $10 - 5 = 5$ $5 + 5 = 10$

2. Megan has 8 flowers.
   She shares 4 flowers with Nick.
   How many flowers do they
   each have?

   What doubles fact helps you?

   _____ − _____ = _____   _____ + _____ = _____

3. Jake has 12 pears.
   He shares 6 pears with Sasha.
   How many pears do they
   each have?

   What doubles fact helps you?

   _____ − _____ = _____   _____ + _____ = _____

4. Jamal has 14 cars.
   He shares 7 cars with Carla.
   How many cars do they
   each have?

   What doubles fact helps you?

   _____ − _____ = _____   _____ + _____ = _____

Name _____

Which Fact?

Circle the addition fact that will help you subtract.
Write a subtraction sentence to solve each problem.

1. Pam has 16 marbles.   16 + 9   8 + 8   7 + 9
   She puts 9 marbles in a jar.
   How many marbles does
   she have out?

   _____ − _____ = _____   Pam has _____ marbles out.

2. Rhonda has 14 baseball cards. 4 + 8   6 + 8   8 + 14
   Chet has 8 baseball cards.
   How many more cards does
   Rhonda have than Chet?

   _____ − _____ = _____   Rhonda has _____ more cards.

3. Marty has 15 stamps.   8 + 7   15 + 6   9 + 6
   He puts 6 stamps in an album.
   How many stamps are not in
   the album?

   _____ − _____ = _____   Marty has _____ stamps out
                             of the album.

4. Lucy has 12 books.   3 + 12   9 + 3   6 + 6
   Michael has 3 books.
   How many more books does
   Lucy have than Michael?

   _____ − _____ = _____   Lucy has _____ more books.

Name _____

What to Buy?

Use the price chart to solve the problems.
Write the number sentence you used.

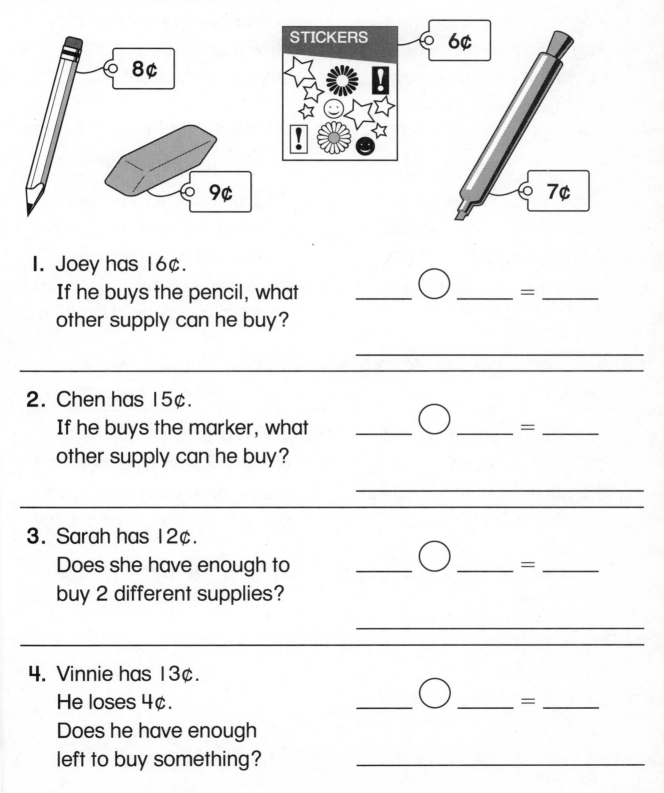

STICKERS 6¢

8¢

9¢

7¢

1. Joey has 16¢.
    If he buys the pencil, what
    other supply can he buy?

    _____ ◯ _____ = _____

    _____

2. Chen has 15¢.
    If he buys the marker, what
    other supply can he buy?

    _____ ◯ _____ = _____

    _____

3. Sarah has 12¢.
    Does she have enough to
    buy 2 different supplies?

    _____ ◯ _____ = _____

    _____

4. Vinnie has 13¢.
    He loses 4¢.
    Does he have enough
    left to buy something?

    _____ ◯ _____ = _____

    _____

At the Farm

Circle the answer that best solves the problem.

1. A hen lays 8 eggs.
   Then she lays some more
   eggs. How many eggs
   could the hen have now?

   15 eggs   7 eggs   5 eggs

2. A cat has 7 kittens.
   Some kittens go off to play.
   How many kittens could
   still be with the cat?

   5 kittens   7 kittens   9 kittens

3. There are 9 horses in the
   field. Some more horses
   come into the field. How
   many horses could be in
   the field now?

   9 horses   8 horses   12 horses

4. A farmer collects 6 pails of
   milk. His wife collects some
   more pails of milk. How
   many pails of milk could
   they have collected in all?

   5 pails   6 pails   9 pails

5. There are 13 cows in the
   barn. Some cows leave
   the barn. How many cows
   could be left in the barn?

   13 cows   8 cows   15 cows

6. There are 12 pigs in the
   pigpen. Some pigs leave
   the pigpen. How many pigs
   could be in the pigpen now?

   15 pigs   6 pigs   12 pigs

What Comes Next?

Find the pattern.
Fill in the pattern that comes next.
Write the number.

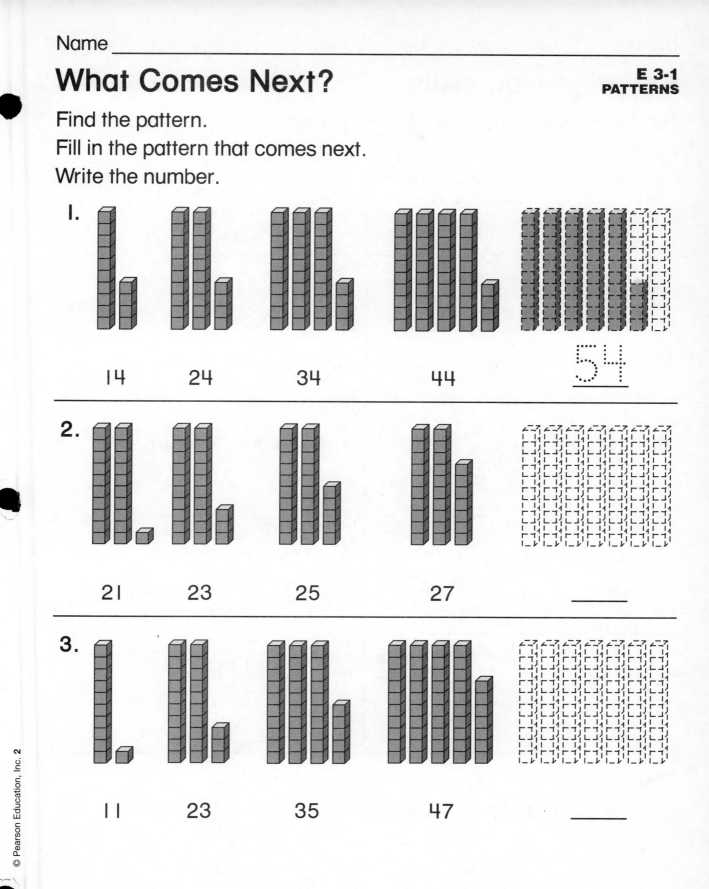

1.

14   24   34   44   54

2.

21   23   25   27   _____

3.

11   23   35   47   _____

Egyptian Numerals

People in Ancient Egypt used these symbols
for numbers.

They used ∩ to show 10. They used ❘ to show 1.	The number 25 looked like this. ∩∩❘❘❘❘❘

Write the number.

1. ∩∩∩❘❘❘❘❘

_____

2. ∩∩∩∩∩

_____

3. ∩❘❘❘❘❘❘❘

_____

4. ∩∩∩∩∩∩❘❘❘

_____

5. ∩∩∩∩∩❘❘❘❘❘❘❘❘

_____

6. ∩∩∩∩∩∩∩❘

_____

7. ❘❘❘❘❘

_____

8. ∩∩❘❘❘❘❘❘❘❘❘

_____

Make up your own symbols for tens and ones.
Use them to write these numbers.

10 is _____.   1 is _____.

9. 51 _____   **10.** 13 _____

Number Match

Draw a line to connect the number to its word name.
Then connect the word name to the tens and ones.

I. 29	sixty-two	4 tens 7 ones
2. 47	twenty-nine	2 tens 9 ones
3. 62	fifty-nine	6 tens 2 ones
4. 19	forty-seven	7 tens 4 ones
5. 95	nineteen	I ten 9 ones
6. 59	thirty	5 tens 9 ones
7. 30	ninety-five	9 tens 5 ones
8. 74	seventy-four	3 tens 0 ones

The letters in these words are all mixed up.
Find the number word.
Then write the number name and the number.

9. esvne _____   _____

10. lwtvee _____   _____

11. ryitth _____   _____

Name _____

Let's Go Riding!

A list can help you see patterns in numbers.
Complete the lists. Then answer the questions.

Bicycles	Wheels
1	2
2	
3	
4	
5	

1. How many wheels
are on 4 bicycles? _____

2. What is the pattern of numbers of
the bicycles?

_____

3. What is the pattern of numbers of
the wheels?

_____

Tricycles	Wheels
1	3
2	
3	
4	
5	

4. How many wheels
are on 5 tricycles? _____

5. What is the pattern of numbers of
the tricycles?

_____

6. What is the pattern of numbers of
the wheels?

_____

7. How could you use a list to show how many
wheels are on 3 wagons?

_____

_____

Kitty Rescue

Choose the number or the symbol from
the tree to complete each exercise.
You may use a number only once.

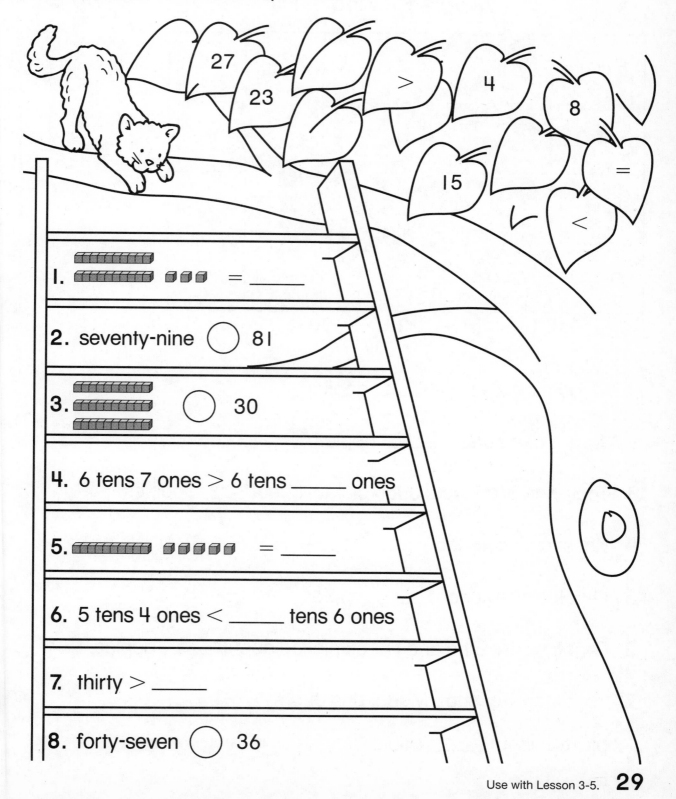

1. ▨▨▨▨▨ ▫▫▫ = _____

2. seventy-nine ◯ 81

3. ▨▨ / ▨▨ / ▨▨ ◯ 30

4. 6 tens 7 ones > 6 tens _____ ones

5. ▨▨▨ ▫▫▫▫▫ = _____

6. 5 tens 4 ones < _____ tens 6 ones

7. thirty > _____

8. forty-seven ◯ 36

Apple Picking Time

Use the graph to find about how many apples were picked.
Write the number of apples to the closest ten.

Apple Picking

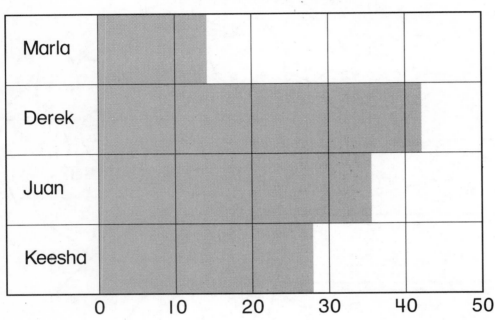

1. Marla picked about _____ apples.

2. Juan picked about _____ apples.

3. Together, Marla and Juan picked about _____ apples.

4. Keesha picked about _____ apples.

5. Derek picked about _____ apples.

6. Together, Keesha and Derek picked about _____ apples.

7. Together, Keesha , Marla, and Juan

   picked about _____ apples.

Hat Tricks

Look at the numbers in the hat.
Use two of the numbers.
Write a two-digit number that will
make the sentence true.

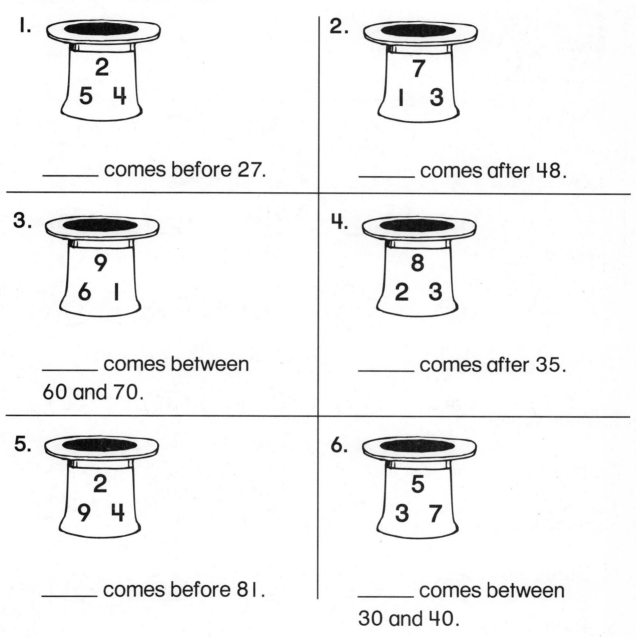

1.
2   5   4

_____ comes before 27.

2.
7   1   3

_____ comes after 48.

3.
9   6   1

_____ comes between
60 and 70.

4.
8   2   3

_____ comes after 35.

5.
2   9   4

_____ comes before 81.

6.
5   3   7

_____ comes between
30 and 40.

Stepping Stones

1. Use a calculator. Press 4 + to help the jaguar
find each stone on the way across the river.
Color each stone the jaguar steps on.

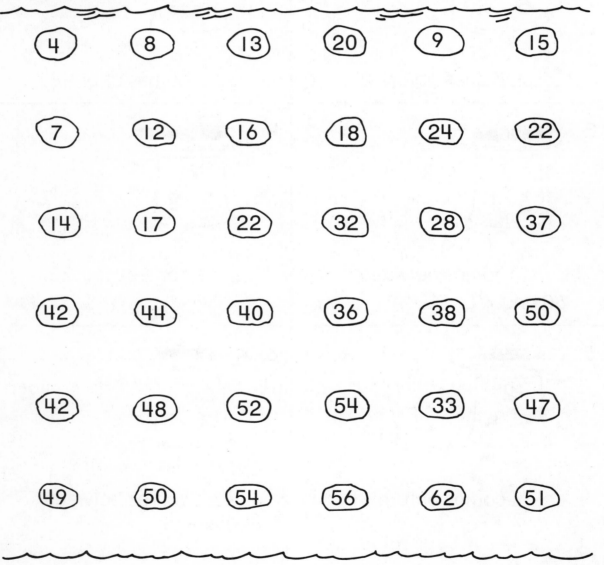

| 4 | 8 | 13 | 20 | 9 | 15 |

| 7 | 12 | 16 | 18 | 24 | 22 |

| 14 | 17 | 22 | 32 | 28 | 37 |

| 42 | 44 | 40 | 36 | 38 | 50 |

| 42 | 48 | 52 | 54 | 33 | 47 |

| 49 | 50 | 54 | 56 | 62 | 51 |

2. Look at the jaguar's path. What is the pattern? _____

Adding Up Odd or Even

Choose the number that will make the sentence true.
Complete the number sentence.

1. The sum is an **odd** number.

5   or   4

$5 + \underline{4} = \underline{9}$

2. The difference is an **even** number.

2   or   3

$8 - \underline{} = \underline{}$

3. The sum is an **even** number.

4   or   5

$9 + \underline{} = \underline{}$

4. The difference is an **odd** number.

8   or   9

$15 - \underline{} = \underline{}$

5. The difference is an **even** number.

6   or   7

$13 - \underline{} = \underline{}$

6. The sum is an **odd** number.

1   or   2

$3 + \underline{} = \underline{}$

Animal Lineup

1. Color the second kitten red.
Make an X on the 9th kitten.

2. Draw a square around the eighth puppy.
Color the 3rd puppy orange.

3. Color the fourth bird yellow.
Draw a circle around the 10th bird.

4. The circle is around the _____ rabbit.

The square is around the _____ rabbit.

Secret Shapes

Use the clues to find the secret shape.

Cross out the shapes on the chart that do not fit the clue.

What is the secret shape?

1. It is not a square.
   It is not a circle.
   It is not in row 3.
   It is in row 4.
   Circle the
   secret shape.

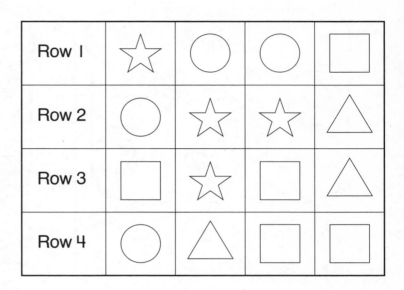

The secret shape is a _____.

What is the secret shape?

2. It is not a square.
   It is not a star.
   It is not in row 4.
   It is in row 2.
   Circle the
   secret shape.

The secret shape is a _____.

Name _____

Which Coins?

Count on to find the total amount in each purse.
Write the total amount.
Then find the missing amount.

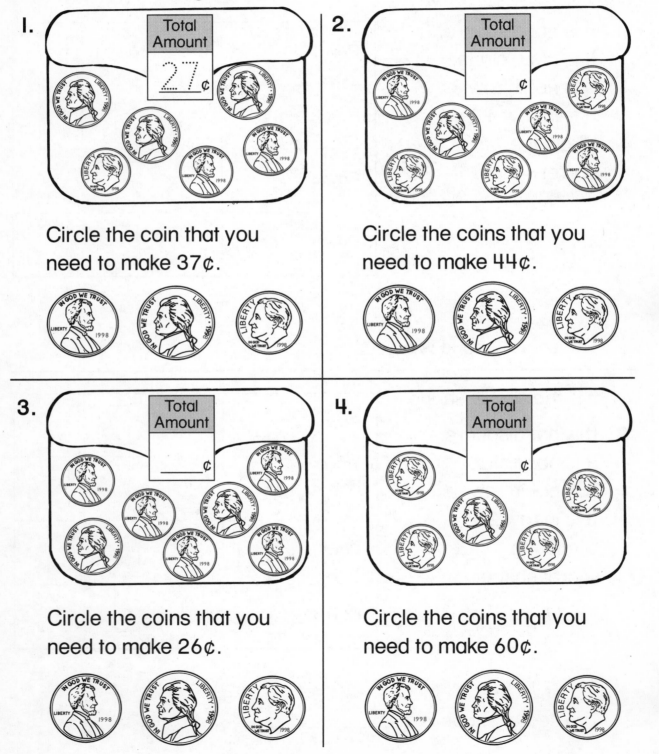

1.

Total Amount

27¢

Circle the coin that you need to make 37¢.

2.

Total Amount

_____ ¢

Circle the coins that you need to make 44¢.

3.

Total Amount

_____ ¢

Circle the coins that you need to make 26¢.

4.

Total Amount

_____ ¢

Circle the coins that you need to make 60¢.

Coin Sense

Find the coins needed to buy the toy.
Write how many coins to use.

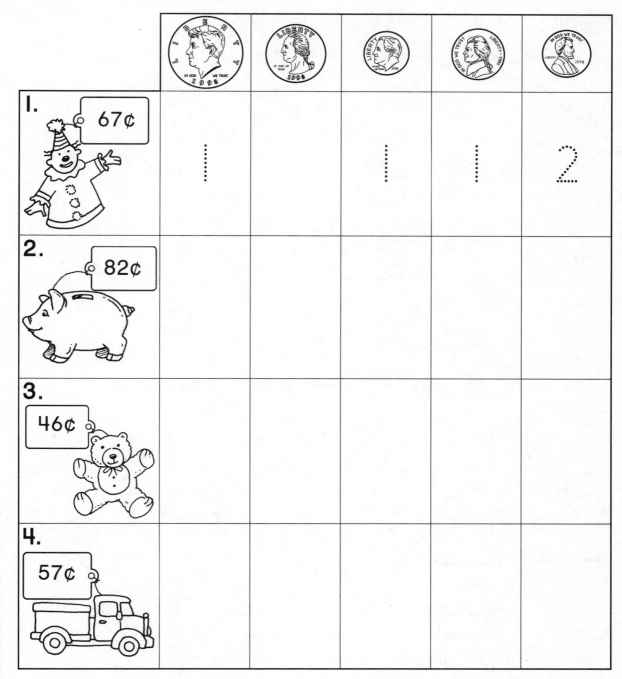

1. 67¢	1		1	1	2
2. 82¢					
3. 46¢					
4. 57¢					

Let's Go Shopping

You have these coins in your piggy bank.

Choose two toys.

Cross out the coins you use to buy each toy.

How much do you have left in your piggy bank? _____

Mystery Coins

1. Shari has 25¢.
Beth also has a coin.
Together they have more than 35¢.
Circle the coin that Beth has.

2. Ahmal has 40¢.
Maya also has a coin.
Together they have less than 60¢.
Circle the coin that Maya has.

3. Ned has 3 dimes.
Marla has a coin too.
Together they have more than 75¢.
Circle the coin that Marla has.

4. Margie has 3 quarters.
Linda has a coin too.
Together they have less than 85¢.
Circle the coin that Linda has.

Coin Count

Circle the correct number of coins to show the amount.

1. Megan has 45¢.
   Circle the 5 coins she has.

2. Yoshi has 45¢
   Circle the 3 coins he has.

3. Kayla has 56¢.
   Circle the 3 coins she has.

4. Peter has 56¢.
   Circle the 6 coins he has.

Name _____

What Is My Change?

Use the chart to answer the questions below.

Circle the coin that is about how much change
each person gets.

1. Amy buys 1 muffin.
   She pays with 50¢.
   About how much is Amy's change?

2. Michael buys 1 carton of milk.
   He pays with 40¢.
   About how much is Michael's change?

3. Jamal buys 1 bowl of soup.
   He pays with 80¢.
   About how much is Jamal's change?

4. Erica buys 1 carton of juice.
   She pays with 50¢.
   About how much is Erica's change?

Name _____

It's All in the Clues

Use the clue cards to complete the chart.
Write how many of each coin.
Write the total amount.

Derek has two coins that equal $1.00.	Roxanne has 10¢ more than Nina. She has 3 coins.	Jamie has one half-dollar.
Nina has 25¢ less than Derek. She has 3 coins.	Elena has 50¢ more than Derek. She has 2 coins.	Todd has 5¢ less than Nina. He has 3 coins.

Child	(half-dollar)	(quarter)	(quarter)	(dime)	(nickel)	Total Amount
1. Derek						
2. Jamie						
3. Nina						
4. Elena						
5. Todd						
6. Roxanne						

Name _____

Mexican Pesos

Many countries have their own kinds of coins and
bills. In Mexico, people use a coin called the peso.
Sometimes people exchange one kind of money
for another. One peso can be exchanged for about
10¢ in United States coins.

Count the pesos. Then answer the questions.

1.

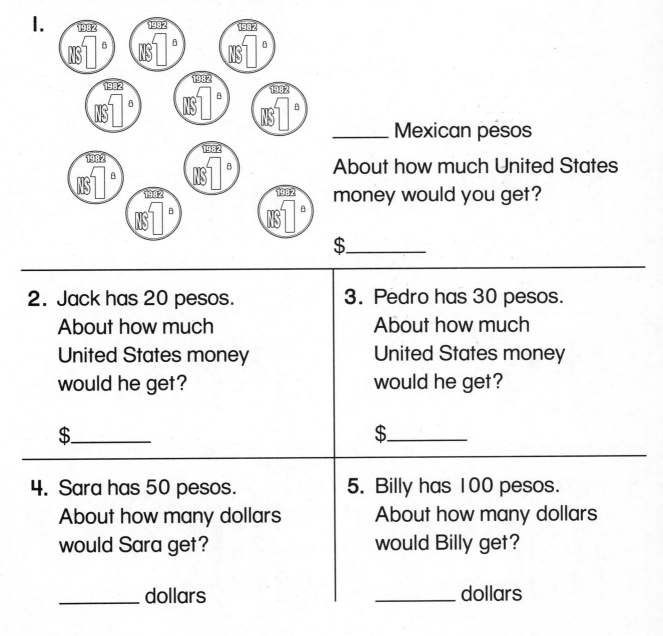

_____ Mexican pesos

About how much United States
money would you get?

$_____

---

2. Jack has 20 pesos.
   About how much
   United States money
   would he get?

   $_____

3. Pedro has 30 pesos.
   About how much
   United States money
   would he get?

   $_____

---

4. Sara has 50 pesos.
   About how many dollars
   would Sara get?

   _____ dollars

5. Billy has 100 pesos.
   About how many dollars
   would Billy get?

   _____ dollars

What's Missing?

Circle the tens that make each addition sentence true.
Then write the number.

1. 35 + _20_ = 55

2. 28 + _____ = 68

3. 42 + _____ = 72

4. 53 + _____ = 63

5. 31 + _____ = 81

6. 36 + _____ = 76

7. 73 + _____ = 93

8. 18 + _____ = 48

Make a Ten

Each triangle can hold ten balls.
Circle the number of balls that will fill the
last triangle to make 10.
Then add all the balls and write the sum.

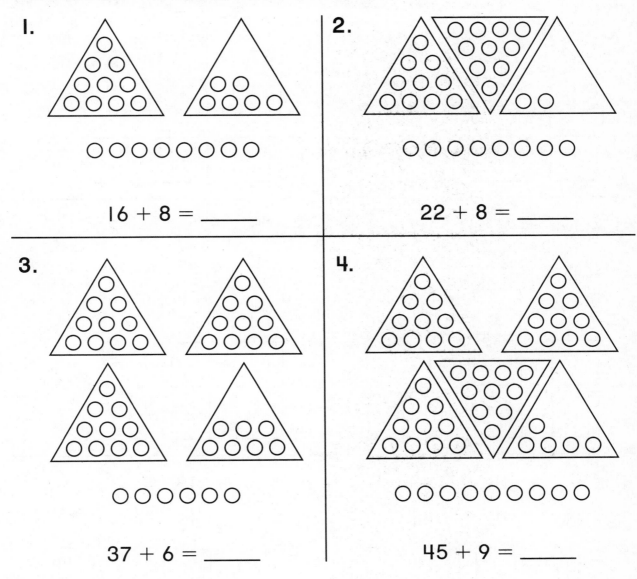

1.

$16 + 8 = $ _____

2.

$22 + 8 = $ _____

3.

$37 + 6 = $ _____

4.

$45 + 9 = $ _____

What Comes Next?

Look at each number pattern.
Write the numbers for the addition sentences that come next.

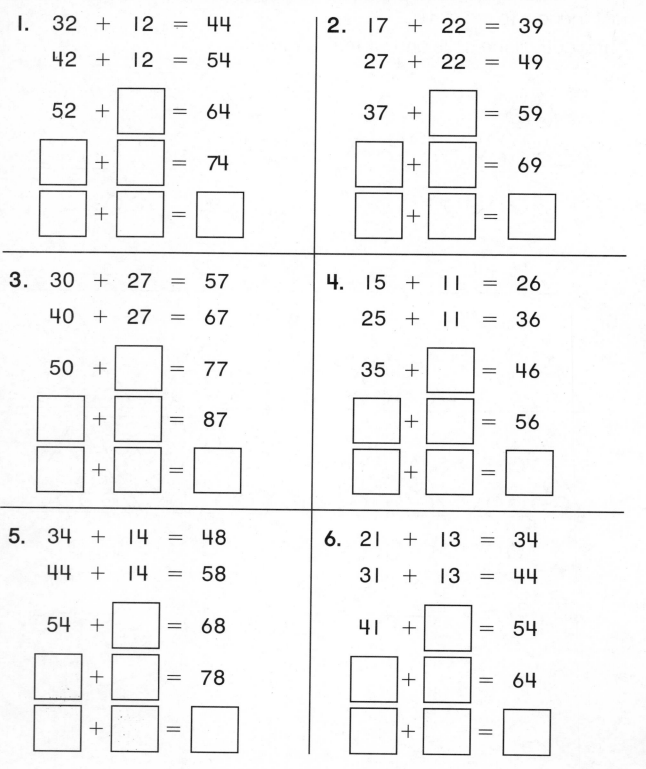

1. 32 + 12 = 44

    42 + 12 = 54

    52 + ☐ = 64

    ☐ + ☐ = 74

    ☐ + ☐ = ☐

2. 17 + 22 = 39

    27 + 22 = 49

    37 + ☐ = 59

    ☐ + ☐ = 69

    ☐ + ☐ = ☐

3. 30 + 27 = 57

    40 + 27 = 67

    50 + ☐ = 77

    ☐ + ☐ = 87

    ☐ + ☐ = ☐

4. 15 + 11 = 26

    25 + 11 = 36

    35 + ☐ = 46

    ☐ + ☐ = 56

    ☐ + ☐ = ☐

5. 34 + 14 = 48

    44 + 14 = 58

    54 + ☐ = 68

    ☐ + ☐ = 78

    ☐ + ☐ = ☐

6. 21 + 13 = 34

    31 + 13 = 44

    41 + ☐ = 54

    ☐ + ☐ = 64

    ☐ + ☐ = ☐

Name _____

Target Practice

Each child threw two bean bags at the target.
Write the number the second bean bag landed on.

1. Allison scores about
50 points. If one bean bag
landed on 32, what number
did the other bean bag
land on?

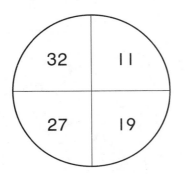

_____

2. Kenji scores about
90 points. If one bean bag
landed on 68, what number
did the other bean bag
land on?

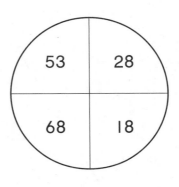

_____

3. Berto scores about
40 points. If one bean bag
landed on 12, what number
did the other bean bag
land on?

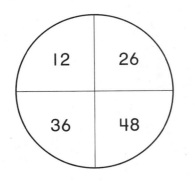

_____

4. Melissa scores about
50 points. If one bean bag
landed on 28, what number
did the other bean bag
land on?

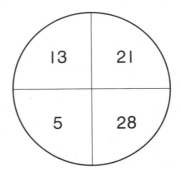

_____

Up the Ladder

Play this game with a partner.
You will need a pencil and a paper clip.

Start at 93. Take turns spinning.
Use the number you spin to subtract.
Then move your piece. The first player
to reach the top of the ladder wins.

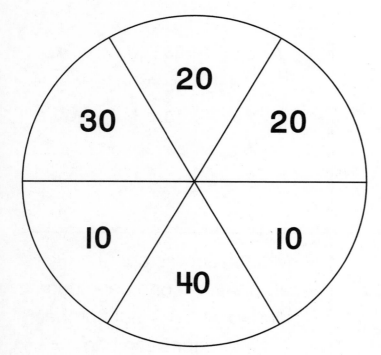

← Start

Name _____

Treasure Chests of Numbers

Look at the numbers in each treasure chest.
Find the missing number to write the subtraction sentence.

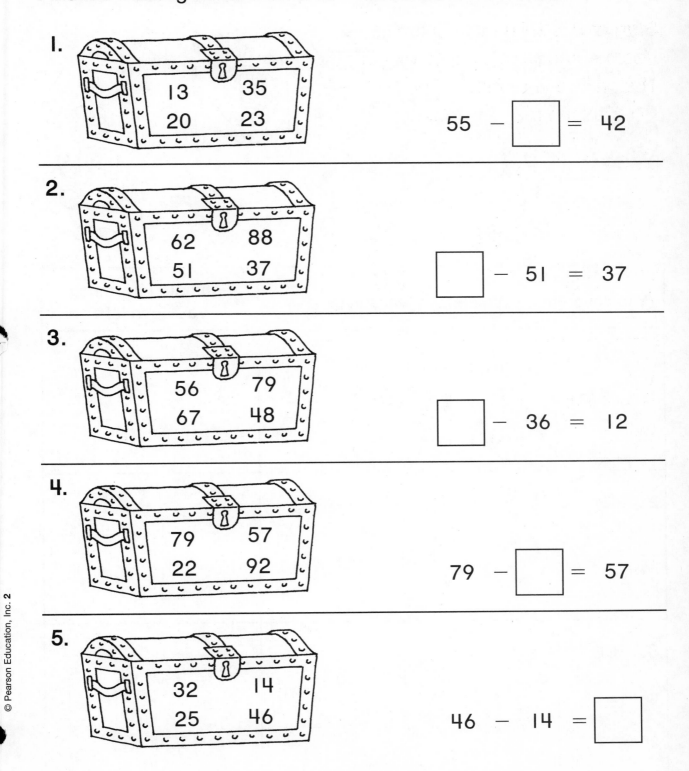

1.

13   35
20   23

$55 - \boxed{} = 42$

2.

62   88
51   37

$\boxed{} - 51 = 37$

3.

56   79
67   48

$\boxed{} - 36 = 12$

4.

79   57
22   92

$79 - \boxed{} = 57$

5.

32   14
25   46

$46 - 14 = \boxed{}$

What Should I Buy?

Circle two toys you will buy.

Estimate to find about how much money you will have left.

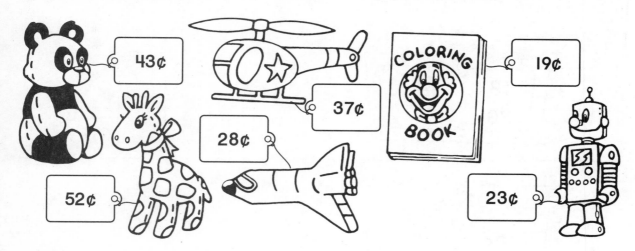

You have	Which toys will you buy?	Estimate how much you have left.
1. 70¢	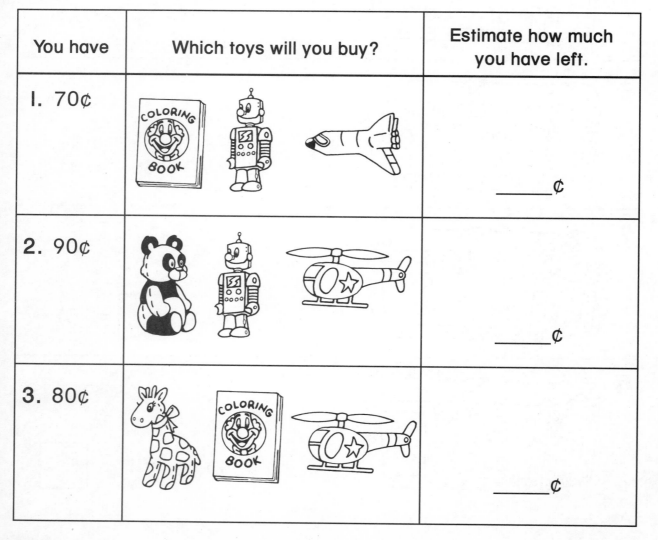	_____ ¢
2. 90¢		_____ ¢
3. 80¢		_____ ¢

At the Fruit Stand

23¢   41¢   36¢   17¢   14¢   29¢   21¢

Which two fruits did each person buy?
Circle the fruits.

1. Marcy spends exactly
   50¢. Which two fruits
   did she buy?

2. Jeremy spends exactly
   40¢. Which two fruits
   did he buy?

3. Ming spends exactly
   70¢. Which two fruits
   did she buy?

4. Leon spends exactly
   50¢. Which two fruits
   did he buy?

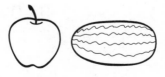

Find the Secret Number

A treasure is hidden under one of the rocks.
Follow the clues to find the treasure.
Color the rocks you land on.

1 2 3 4 5 6 7 8 9 10
11 12 13 14 15 16 17 18 19 20
21 22 23 24 25 26 27 28 29 30
31 32 33 34 35 36 37 38 39 40
41 42 43 44 45 46 47 48 49 50
51 52 53 54 55 56 57 58 59 60
61 62 63 64 65 66 67 68 69 70
71 72 73 74 75 76 77 78 79 80

1. Start at 55.   2. Subtract 20.

3. Add 5.   4. Add 20.

5. Add 10.   6. Subtract 5.

7. Subtract 20.   8. Add 5.

9. Subtract 20.   10. Subtract 5.

11. Under which rock is the treasure hidden? _____

12. Write the pattern you see in the numbers you colored.

_____

Missing Parts

Circle the basket that makes the other part of 100.
Write the number.

1. 25   and   25   and _____ is 100.

    25 and 25 and _____

    50   30

2. 30   and   30   and _____ is 100.

    30 and 30 and _____

    30   40

3. 10   and   45   and _____ is 100.

    10 and 45 and _____

    50   45

4. 15   and   60   and _____ is 100.

    15 and 60 and _____

    20   25

5. 40   and   25   and _____ is 100.

    40 and 25 and _____

    35   25

Name _____

Look Back and Check

Circle the most reasonable answer.

1. There are 12 children at a party. More children come to the party. How many children could be at the party now?

Tell why you chose your answer.

   12 children

   6 children

   15 children

_____

_____

2. There are 15 people at a picnic. Some people leave to go home. How many people could be at the picnic now?

Tell why you chose your answer.

   11 people

   15 people

   18 people

_____

_____

3. Bridget has 26 stickers. She gives some stickers to her little brother. How many stickers could Bridget's little brother have?

Tell why you chose your answer.

   26 stickers

   8 stickers

   30 stickers

_____

_____

Batter Up

Use the chart to solve the problems below.

Home Runs Hit by the Bluebirds Baseball Team

Mickey	Shawna	Jose	Benji	Chrissy	Billy
28	14	31	9	18	36

1. How many home runs did Mickey and Benji hit altogether?

_____ home runs

2. How many more home runs did Billy hit than Chrissy?

_____ home runs

3. Suppose Jose hits 5 more home runs. How many home runs would he have now?

_____ home runs

4. How many home runs did Mickey and Jose hit altogether?

_____ home runs

5. Who hit the most home runs? How many more home runs did that person hit than Shawna?

_____ hit the most home runs.

_____ more home runs than Shawna

6. Who hit the least home runs? How many fewer home runs did that person hit than Mickey?

_____ hit the least home runs.

_____ less home runs than Mickey

Name _____

Which Team?

Decide if you need to regroup. Color the shirts
red if you do. Color the shirts blue if you don't.
Find each sum and write the number on the shirt.

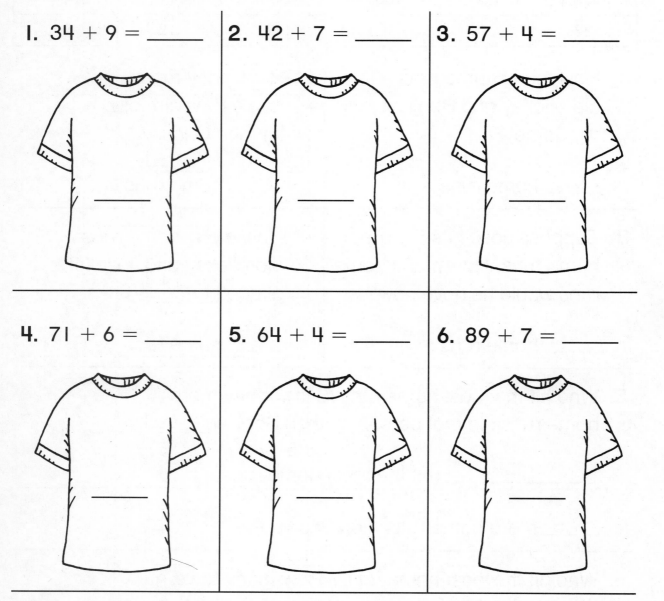

1. 34 + 9 = _____

2. 42 + 7 = _____

3. 57 + 4 = _____

4. 71 + 6 = _____

5. 64 + 4 = _____

6. 89 + 7 = _____

7. Write the numbers of each shirt under the correct team.

Red Team	Blue Team

Which Number Will You Add?

Look for a pattern in each row. Circle the number
that will make each addition problem true.

1.

46	56	66	76	6
+ ☐	+ ☐	+ ☐	+ ☐	
5 2	6 2	7 2	8 2	7

2.

2 1	3 1	4 1	5 1	4
+ ☐	+ ☐	+ ☐	+ ☐	
2 6	3 6	4 6	5 6	5

3.

3 5	4 5	5 5	6 5	8
+ ☐	+ ☐	+ ☐	+ ☐	
4 4	5 4	6 4	7 4	9

4.

5 8	6 8	7 8	8 8	7
+ ☐	+ ☐	+ ☐	+ ☐	
6 5	7 5	8 5	9 5	8

5.

4 9	5 9	6 9	7 9	3
+ ☐	+ ☐	+ ☐	+ ☐	
5 3	6 3	7 3	8 3	4

Empty Circles

Write the number in the circle to complete each addition problem.

1.

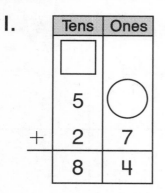

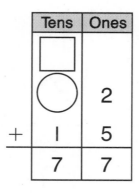

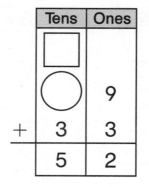

2.

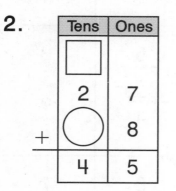

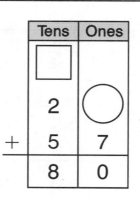

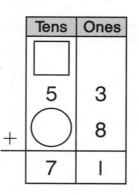

3.

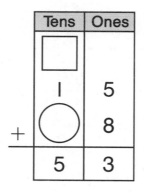

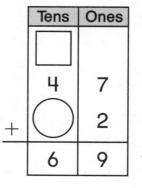

Name _____

Pathways Through the Farm

Use the map to write each problem. Add.
Use tens and ones models if you like.

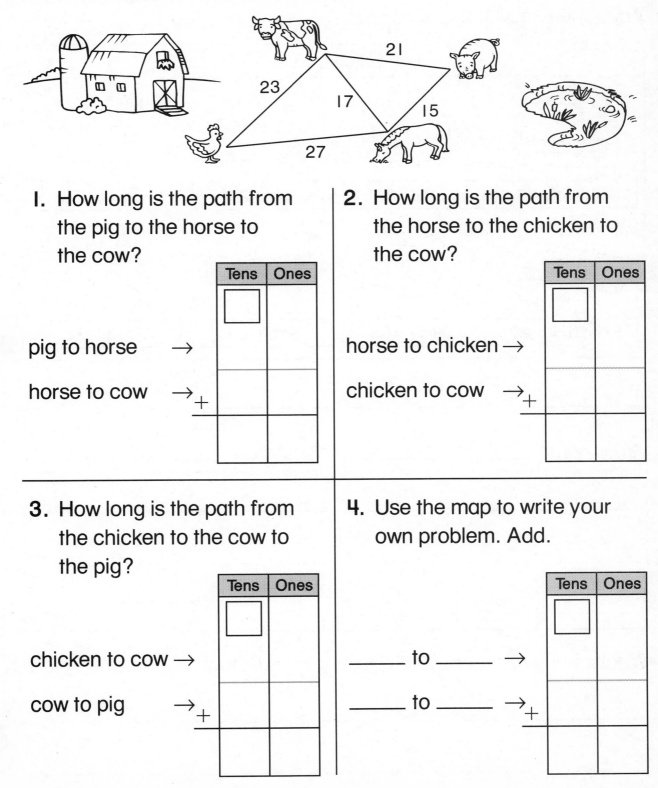

1. How long is the path from the pig to the horse to the cow?

pig to horse   →

horse to cow   →
+

Tens	Ones
☐	

2. How long is the path from the horse to the chicken to the cow?

horse to chicken →

chicken to cow   →
+

Tens	Ones
☐	

3. How long is the path from the chicken to the cow to the pig?

chicken to cow →

cow to pig   →
+

Tens	Ones
☐	

4. Use the map to write your own problem. Add.

_____ to _____ →

_____ to _____ →
+

Tens	Ones
☐	

Name _____

Lunch Time!

Write your name and a classmate's name.

Write 2 things each of you would like for lunch.

Add. Then answer the questions.

Lunch Menu

Sandwich 47¢   Milk 18¢   Soup 24¢   Yogurt 35¢

Granola Bar 29¢   Juice 15¢   Salad 20¢   Pizza 42¢

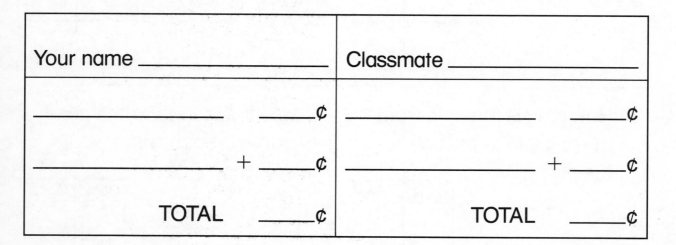

Your name _____	Classmate _____
_____ ____¢	_____ ____¢
_____ + ____¢	_____ + ____¢
TOTAL ____¢	TOTAL ____¢

Who spent more money? Explain how you know.

_____

Name _____

It's in the Clues

Three of the numbers added make the sum.
Read the clues to help you.
Circle the three numbers.
Check by adding to find the sum.

1. Sum 83   5   44   12   19   10   20

One number is the sum of $22 + 22$.
One number is one less than 20.
One number is greater than 19 and less than 44.

$+$
_____

_____

2. Sum 72   36   12   25   7   33   14

One number has the same number in both digits.
One number is more than 12 and less than 25.
One number is 20 more than 5.

$+$
_____

_____

3. Sum 80   29   19   49   12   20   11

One number is 8 less than 20.
One number is the sum of $24 + 25$.
One number is more than 12 and less than 20.

$+$
_____

_____

4. Sum 88   24   31   17   43   28   35

One number is the sum of $14 + 14$.
One number has the greatest value.
One number is 9 more than 8.

$+$
_____

Favorite Animals in the Wild

Use the data from the table to solve each problem.
Use paper and pencil to show your work.

Favorite Wild Animals					
	Lion	Elephant	Monkey	Zebra	Giraffe
Grade 1	24	16	13	8	11
Grade 2	16	9	26	19	21

1. Write the total number of votes for each wild animal.

   Lion   Elephant   Monkey   Zebra   Giraffe

   _____   _____   _____   _____   _____

2. Draw a red circle around the name of the animal that has the most votes.

3. Draw a blue circle around the name of the animal that has the least votes.

4. How many children voted for lions and zebras in Grade 2?

   _____

5. How many children voted for elephants, monkeys, and giraffes in Grade 1?

   _____

Card Collections

The chart shows how many sports cards each child collects. Use the chart to estimate your answers.
Circle the closest ten.

	Jason	Linda	Cora	Roberto
Baseball	28	19	43	34
Football	34	22	17	57

About how many baseball and football cards does each child have?

1. Cora	60	70	80
2. Jason	50	60	70
3. Roberto	80	90	100
4. Linda	30	40	50

5. About how many football cards do Jason and Cora have in all?	40	50	60
6. About how many baseball cards do Linda and Roberto have in all?	40	50	60

Name _____

Sum Boxes

Circle all the number pairs in each box that equal the sum above it. Then write the way you solved the problem.

- mental math
- paper and pencil
- cubes
- calculator

1. Sum 22

10	4	18
12	15	14
22	21	13

_____

2. Sum 55

25	30	14
18	14	45
15	21	10

_____

3. Sum 83

30	45	30
56	19	64
27	29	20

_____

4. Sum 40

33	7	26
10	24	16
18	4	9

_____

Name _____

Bean Bag Champs

Each child gets two tosses. Shade the squares on each game board that could show what each child might have tossed.

1. Benji scores about 50 points.

12	32
46	19

2. Terry scores about 80 points.

18	27
52	43

3. Zack scores about 70 points.

43	28
21	17

4. Mindy scores about 40 points.

12	38
22	26

5. Leroy scores about 60 points.

38	46
21	32

6. Yuki scores about 90 points.

18	14
13	67

Name _____

How Tall?

Mr. Reynolds's second grade class grew some plants. Every week, they measured the plants to see how much they grew. Here is a chart showing the plant growth. Use the chart to answer the questions.

Plant Growth in Centimeters

Week	1	2	3	4
Plant A	2	1	3	1
Plant B	2	4	3	2
Plant C	3	5	2	6

1. How many centimeters did plant A grow during weeks 2 and 3?

   _____ centimeters

2. How many centimeters did plant C grow during weeks 1 and 2?

   _____ centimeters

3. If plant B continues to grow 2 centimeters every week, how tall will it be during week 6?

   _____ centimeters tall

4. What was the total number for plant growth for all three plants during week 4?

   _____ centimeters

5. Which plant is the tallest, plant A or plant B? Explain how you know.

   _____

   _____

Pick A Number

Choose a number from the chart to subtract.
Cross out each number you choose.
Write the number in the box.
Decide if you need to regroup. Subtract.
You may use each number only once.

3	5	1	9	4	7	2	8	6

Did you regroup?

1. $62 - \boxed{} = $ _____   yes   no

2. $45 - \boxed{} = $ _____   yes   no

3. $71 - \boxed{} = $ _____   yes   no

4. $34 - \boxed{} = $ _____   yes   no

5. $82 - \boxed{} = $ _____   yes   no

6. $90 - \boxed{} = $ _____   yes   no

7. $58 - \boxed{} = $ _____   yes   no

Name _____

Pet Stickers

The children put pet stickers in notebooks.
Subtract to find how many stickers there are left.

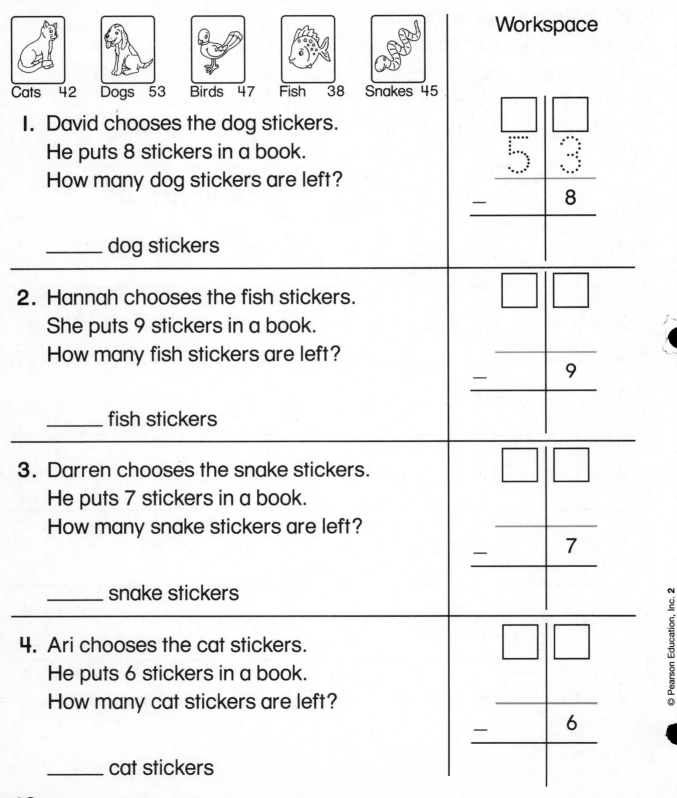

Cats 42   Dogs 53   Birds 47   Fish 38   Snakes 45

Workspace

1. David chooses the dog stickers.
He puts 8 stickers in a book.
How many dog stickers are left?

```
 5  3
-    8
```

_____ dog stickers

2. Hannah chooses the fish stickers.
She puts 9 stickers in a book.
How many fish stickers are left?

```
-    9
```

_____ fish stickers

3. Darren chooses the snake stickers.
He puts 7 stickers in a book.
How many snake stickers are left?

```
-    7
```

_____ snake stickers

4. Ari chooses the cat stickers.
He puts 6 stickers in a book.
How many cat stickers are left?

```
-    6
```

_____ cat stickers

Solve the Mystery

Use the numbers above each exercise
to make the subtraction problem true.
Write the numbers in the circles.

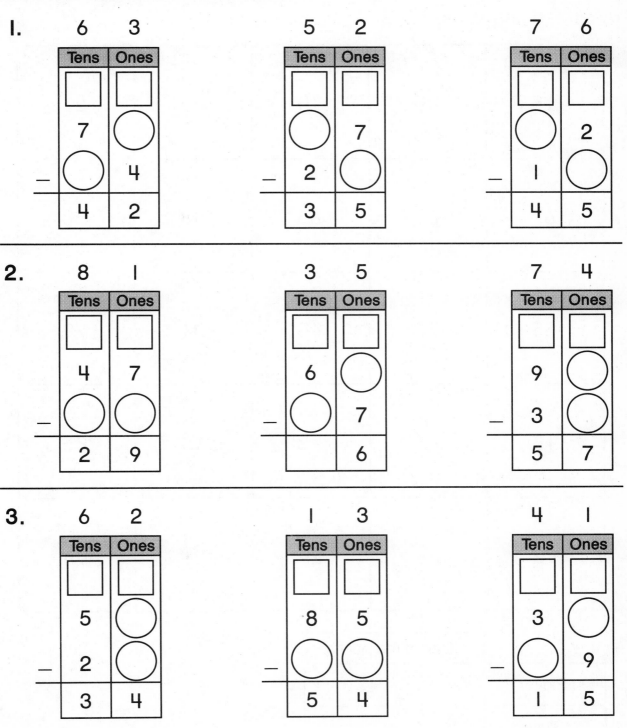

1.

6 3

Tens	Ones
☐	☐
7	◯
◯	4
4	2

5 2

Tens	Ones
☐	☐
◯	7
2	◯
3	5

7 6

Tens	Ones
☐	☐
◯	2
1	◯
4	5

2.

8 1

Tens	Ones
☐	☐
4	7
◯	◯
2	9

3 5

Tens	Ones
☐	☐
6	◯
◯	7
	6

7 4

Tens	Ones
☐	☐
9	◯
3	◯
5	7

3.

6 2

Tens	Ones
☐	☐
5	◯
2	◯
3	4

1 3

Tens	Ones
☐	☐
8	5
◯	◯
5	4

4 1

Tens	Ones
☐	☐
3	◯
◯	9
1	5

5-Points

Play with a partner. Take turns. Choose two numbers.
Subtract. The player with the greater difference gets
1 point. Cross out the numbers used. The first player
to get 5 points wins.

15	46	14	73	27
67	23	65	98	50
35	77	80	41	79
12	61	43	54	85
92	39	29	31	96

	Record the points
1st Player	
2nd Player	

Name _____

Butterfly Collections

The chart shows the number of butterflies each child collects.
Write a number sentence to solve the problem.
Use the data in the chart. Show your work.

Number of Butterflies in a Collection					
Jimmy	Lucas	Anna	Mario	Yuki	Ruth
14	35	27	52	41	22

Workspace

1. How many more butterflies does Yuki
have than Jimmy?

   _____ ◯ _____ = _____ more butterflies

Tens	Ones

2. How many butterflies do Anna and
Lucas have in all?

   _____ ◯ _____ = _____ in all

Tens	Ones

3. Mario gives 16 butterflies to Ruth.
How many butterflies does Mario have left?

   _____ ◯ _____ = _____ butterflies left

Tens	Ones

Name _____

Shopping Day

Decide what each child will buy.
Subtract to find how much money is left.

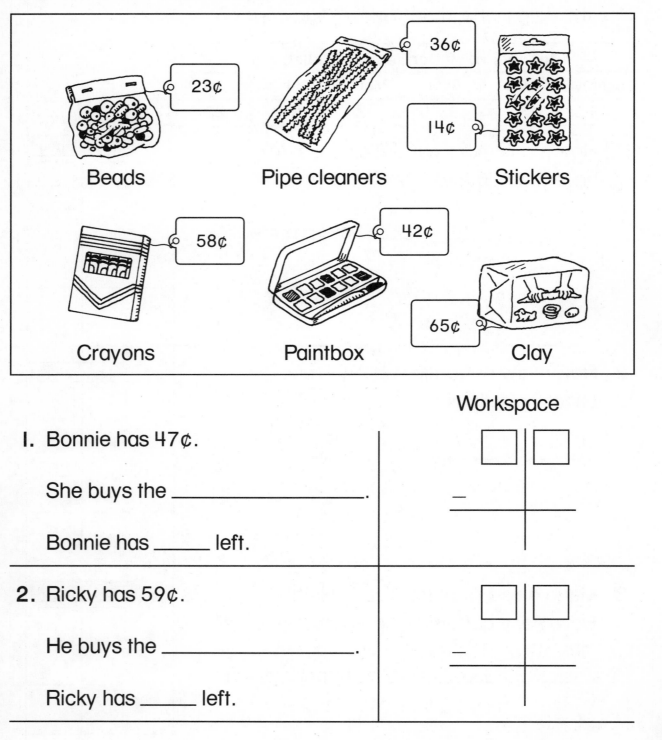

Beads 23¢ Pipe cleaners 36¢ Stickers 14¢

Crayons 58¢ Paintbox 42¢ Clay 65¢

Workspace

I. Bonnie has 47¢.

She buys the _____.

Bonnie has _____ left.

☐ ☐
–

2. Ricky has 59¢.

He buys the _____.

Ricky has _____ left.

☐ ☐
–

3. Which item is the one that neither child can buy? _____

At the Check-Out

Subtract. Check your answer by adding.

	Subtract	Check
1. Mei Ling has 71¢. She spent 25¢. How much money does Mei Ling have left?		
2. Eric has 62¢. He spent 33¢. How much money does Eric have left?		
3. Dennis has 51¢. He spent 32¢. How much money does Dennis have left?		
4. Raul has 99¢. He spent 49¢. How much money does Raul have left?		

Yard Sale

Teapot **26¢**

Lunchbox **42¢**

Vase **39¢**

Pot **54¢**

Choose the items each person buys at the yard sale.

Find the closest 10 to estimate how much money is left.

Workspace

I. Don has 67¢. What does he buy?

_____

Don has about _____ ¢ left.

2. Millie has 80¢. What does she buy?

_____

Millie has about _____ ¢ left.

3. Stefan has 72¢. What does he buy?

_____

Stefan has about _____ ¢ left.

Secret Numbers

Use the numbers in the chart to solve each problem.
Did you use mental math, cubes, paper and pencil,
or a calculator? Write the way you solved the problem.

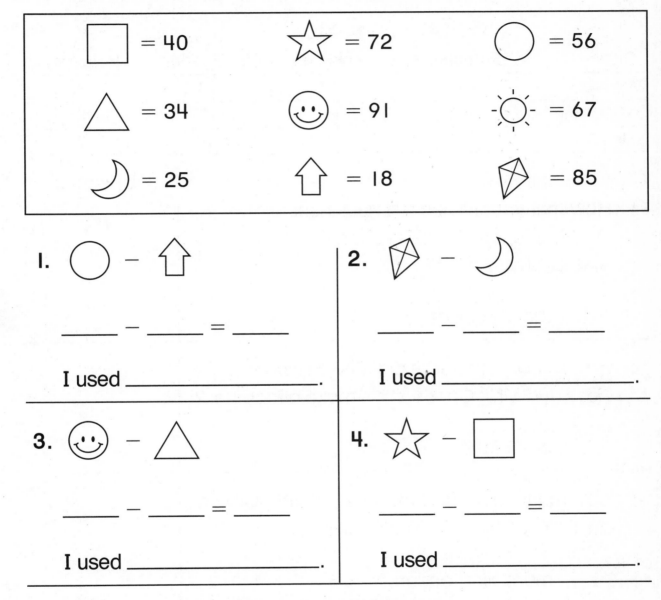

□ = 40   ☆ = 72   ◯ = 56

△ = 34   ☺ = 91   ☀ = 67

☽ = 25   ⬆ = 18   ◇ = 85

1. ◯ – ⬆

_____ – _____ = _____

I used _____.

2. ◇ – ☽

_____ – _____ = _____

I used _____.

3. ☺ – △

_____ – _____ = _____

I used _____.

4. ☆ – □

_____ – _____ = _____

I used _____.

5. Use the shapes in the chart. Write your own
secret number sentence. Then solve.

_____ – _____   _____ – _____ = _____

Meet Me at the Crafts Fair

Three classes made crafts for the fair.
Cross out the extra information in the chart.
Then solve the problems.

Class	Potholders	Necklaces	Bird Feeders	Puppets
Mr. Mark's	17	42	13	14
Miss Brown's	21	18	19	12
Mrs. Cruz's	25	32	31	18

Workspace

1. How many more beaded necklaces
   did Mr. Mark's class make than
   Miss Brown's class?

   _____ more necklaces

2. How many potholders did Miss Brown's
   class and Mrs. Cruz's class make altogether?

   _____ potholders

3. How many more bird feeders did Mrs. Cruz's
   class make than Mr. Mark's class?

   _____ more bird feeders

4. How many potholders did Mr. Mark's class
   and Miss Brown's class make in all?

   _____ potholders

Animal Safari

Mr. and Mrs. Santos went
on an African safari. Use the
information in the chart to
answer the questions.

Number of Animals Seen		
	Day 1	Day 2
Giraffes	65	27
Elephants	9	32
Lions	16	25
Zebras	11	48

1. How many more giraffes did the Santos's
   see on Day 1 than on Day 2?

   _____ ◯ _____ = _____ more giraffes

2. How many more elephants than giraffes
   did they see on Day 2?

   _____ ◯ _____ = _____ more elephants

3. Which number would be the
   most reasonable estimate for the
   number of lions they saw in all?

   30   40   50

4. How many more zebras than lions did
   they see on Day 2?

   _____ ◯ _____ = _____ more zebras

Two Solids Make One

Circle the 2 solid figures that make the first object.
Draw the missing edge that connects the solids.

1.

2.

3.

4.

A Shape Graph

Count the number of circles, squares, rectangles, and triangles that are made by tracing each flat surface of each solid. Color one box in the graph for every plane shape you count.

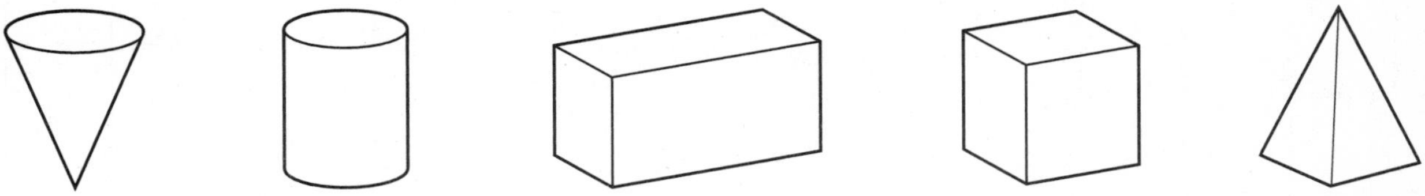

Number of Plane Shapes Found in Solids										
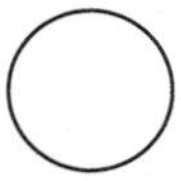 ○										
□										
 △										
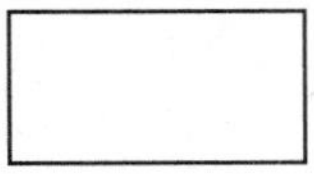 ▭										
	1	2	3	4	5	6	7	8	9	10

Answer the questions.

1. Write the total number of plane shapes counted.

   _3_ circles   _____ squares

   _____ rectangles   _____ triangles

2. Which plane shape was counted the most? _____

3. Which plane shape was counted the least? _____

All Kinds of Nets

Write the name of the solid figure you could form
from each net. Then answer the questions.

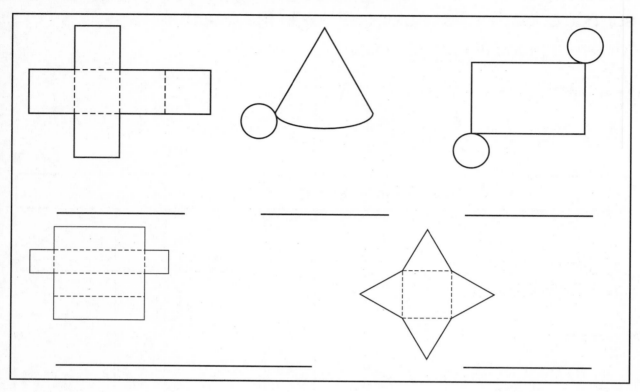

_____   _____   _____

_____   _____

1. How many folds does it take to make a pyramid? _____

2. Which two figures could you form by making 5 folds?

_____

_____

3. Name two figures you could make with nets
   that contain circles.

_____

_____

4. Which figures have nets that contain squares?

_____

Make a Shape

Use pattern blocks to make the shape.
Trace and color to show one way.

1. Use 6 blocks.

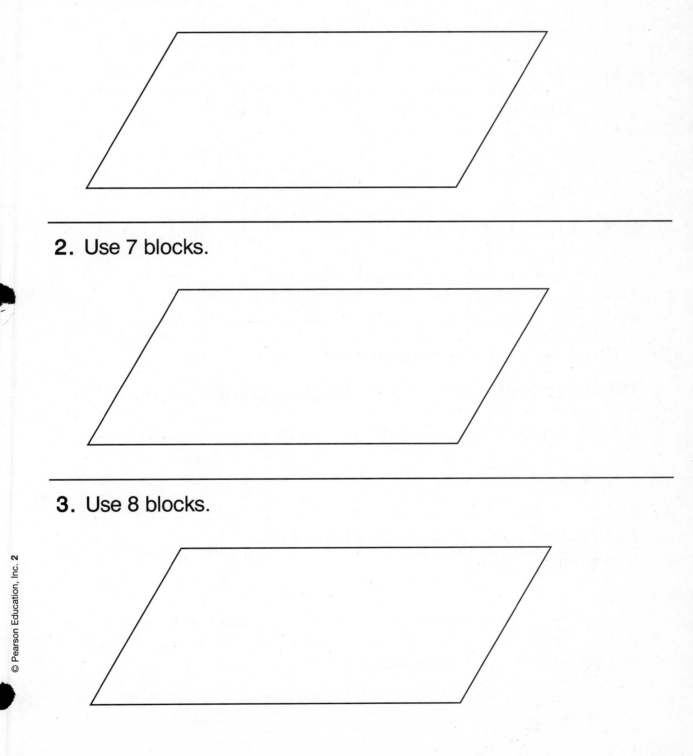

2. Use 7 blocks.

3. Use 8 blocks.

Same and Different

Draw 2 shapes that are congruent.

1. Draw triangles.

2. Draw trapezoids.

Draw 2 shapes that are not congruent.

3. Draw hexagons.

4. Draw parallelograms.

Crazy Letters

Do the letters show a flip, a slide, or a turn?
Circle what comes next.

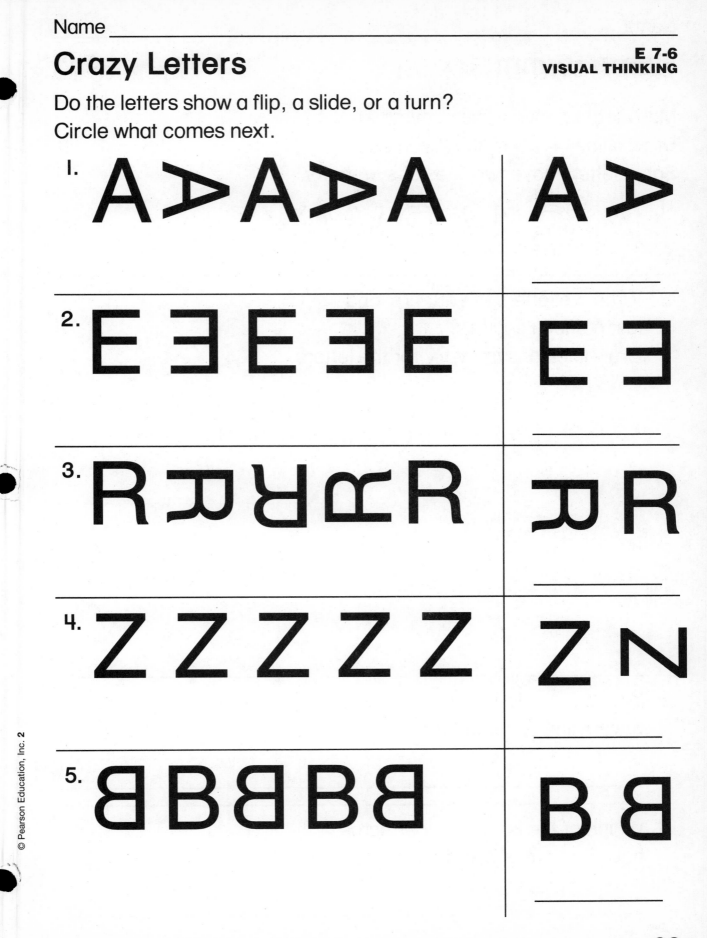

Name _____

Name Symmetry

Many letters have a line of symmetry.
Draw a line of symmetry if you can.
Some letters have two lines of symmetry.

1.

2. Write the letters of your first and
last name in capitals.
Draw lines of symmetry for the letters.

3. Which of the letters in your name
have 1 line of symmetry?

_____

4. Which of the letters in your name
have no lines of symmetry?

_____

Solid Shape Riddles

Read the clues.

Circle the solid shape that answers the question.

1. Who am I?

My flat surfaces are circles.

I have 0 edges.

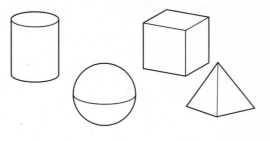

2. Who am I?

One of my flat surfaces
is a square.

I have 5 vertices.

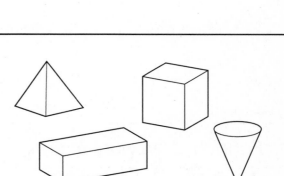

3. Who am I?

My flat surface is a circle.

I have 0 edges.

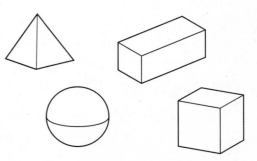

4. Who am I?

I have more than 8 edges.

Only 2 of my faces are squares.

Let's Share Lunch

1. Two children want to share a small pizza. Draw two ways to split the pizza into halves.

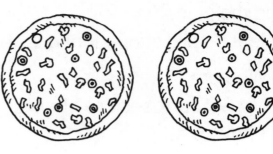

2. Three children want to share a tray of apple crisp. Draw two ways to split the apple crisp into thirds.

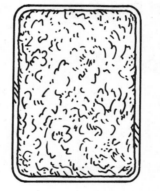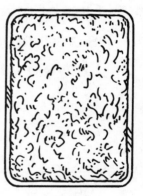

3. Four children want to share an apple pie. Draw lines to split the pie into fourths.

Shapes of Color

Each shape is divided into equal parts.

Color 1 part red.

Write the fraction for the part that is red.

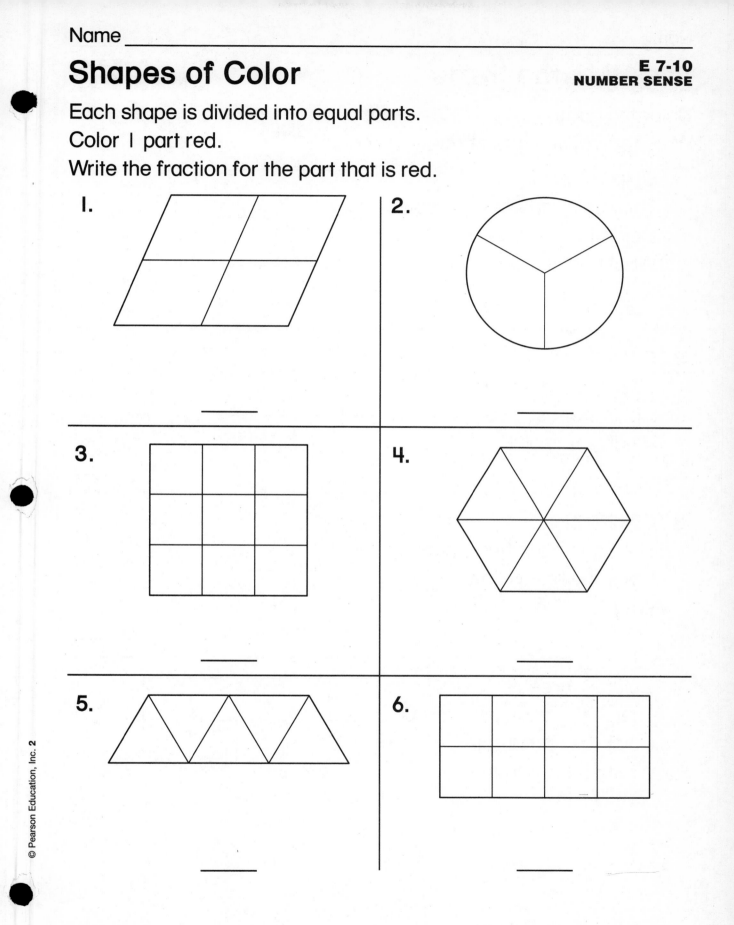

1.

2.

_____

_____

3.

4.

_____

_____

5.

6.

_____

_____

It's All in the Parts

Color the parts.

Write the fraction for the parts you color.

1. Color $\frac{1}{8}$ yellow.
   Then color another $\frac{2}{8}$ yellow.
   Color the rest green.
   What part is green?

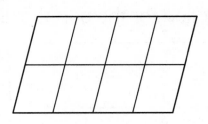

_____

2. Color $\frac{2}{5}$ red.
   Then color another $\frac{1}{5}$ red.
   Color the rest blue.
   What part is blue?

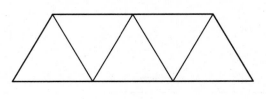

_____

3. Color $\frac{1}{6}$ pink.
   Then color another $\frac{3}{6}$ pink.
   Color the rest yellow.
   What part is yellow?

_____

4. Color $\frac{4}{10}$ green.
   Then color another $\frac{2}{10}$ green.
   Color the rest purple.
   What part is purple?

_____

Oodles of Noodles

About how much is needed
to fill each jar to the fill line?
Circle your answer.

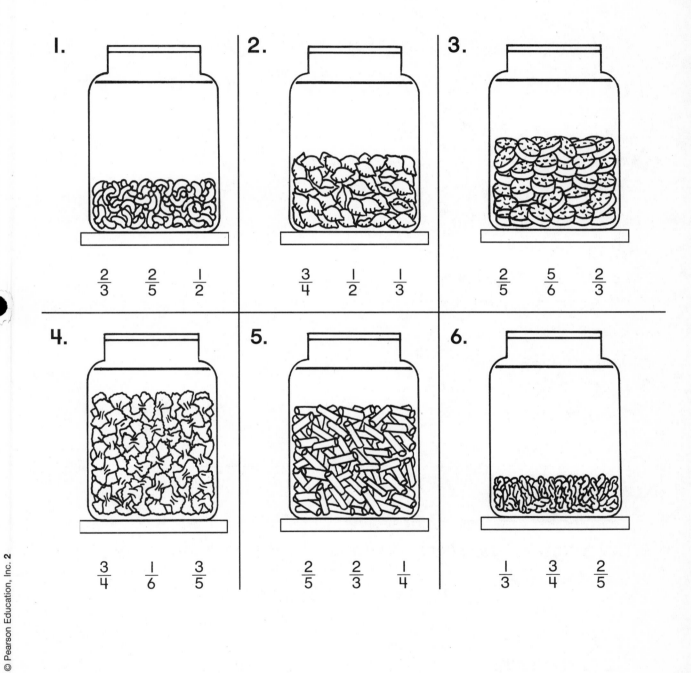

1. $\frac{2}{3}$ $\frac{2}{5}$ $\frac{1}{2}$

2. $\frac{3}{4}$ $\frac{1}{2}$ $\frac{1}{3}$

3. $\frac{2}{5}$ $\frac{5}{6}$ $\frac{2}{3}$

4. $\frac{3}{4}$ $\frac{1}{6}$ $\frac{3}{5}$

5. $\frac{2}{5}$ $\frac{2}{3}$ $\frac{1}{4}$

6. $\frac{1}{3}$ $\frac{3}{4}$ $\frac{2}{5}$

Making Fruit Salad

Make fruit salad. Color a part of each group
of fruit. Write the fraction. Then write your
recipe for fruit salad below.

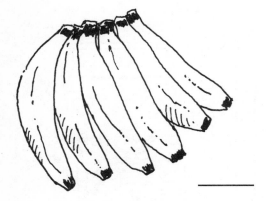

_____

_____

_____   _____

_____

Tell how many of each fruit you chose. Write the fraction.

My Recipe for Fruit Salad

_____ bananas   _____ grapes

_____ strawberries   _____ cherries

Shell Shaped Animals

Some animals have shells that
protect their bodies.
Use the animals in the pictures
to answer your questions.

| Fiddler crab | Snail | Turtle | Horseshoe crab |

1. Draw a line of symmetry for each animal that you can.
   Which animals are symmetrical?

   _____

2. Which animals have a rounded shape?

   _____

3. Which animals have shells shaped like an oval? $\bigcirc$

   _____

4. Which animal has legs that are shaped like cylinders?

   _____

Just 5 More Minutes

Draw hands on the clock to show the time
5 minutes later. Then write the time.

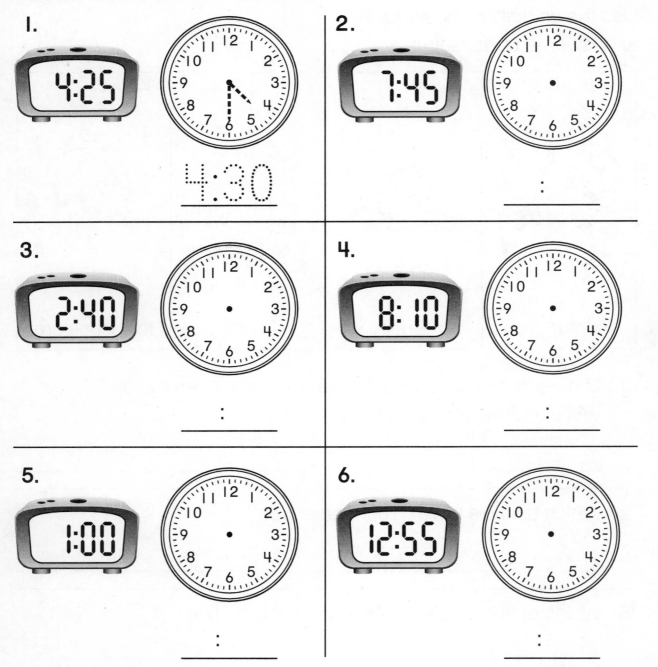

1.

4:25

4·30

2.

7:45

:

3.

2:40

:

4.

8:10

:

5.

1:00

:

6.

12:55

:

© Pearson Education, Inc. 2

What's the Time?

Look for a pattern.
Write the missing time. Then write
another way to say the time.

1.

_____

2.

_____

3.

_____

Early, Late, or On Time?

Write the time.
Then answer each question.

1. Nancy arrives at 10 minutes before 8.

   _____

   School starts at

   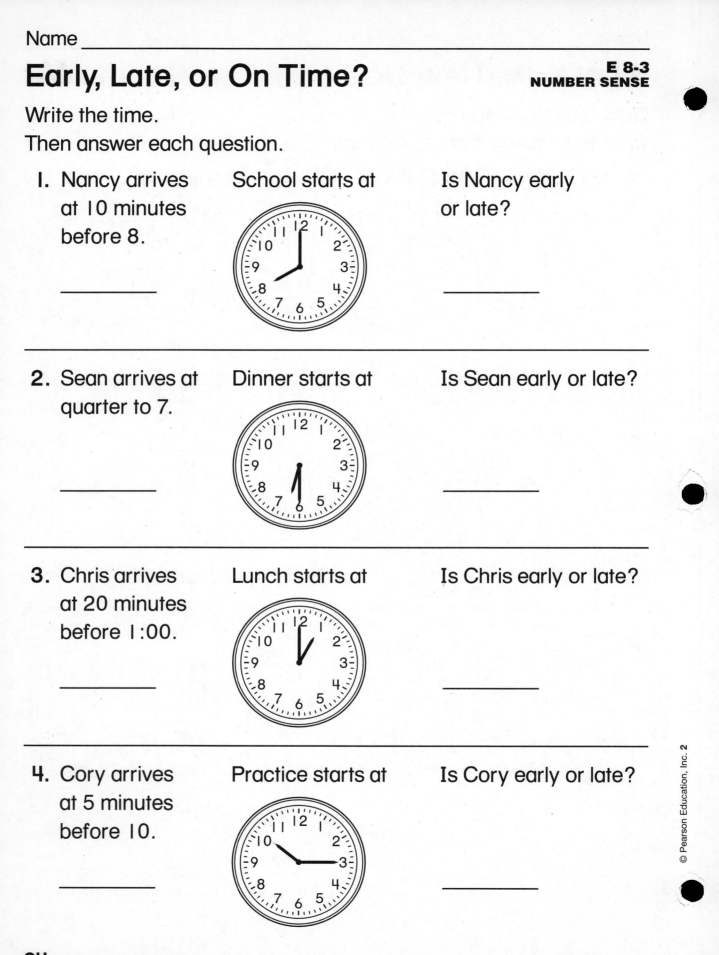

   Is Nancy early or late?

   _____

2. Sean arrives at quarter to 7.

   _____

   Dinner starts at

   Is Sean early or late?

   _____

3. Chris arrives at 20 minutes before 1:00.

   _____

   Lunch starts at

   Is Chris early or late?

   _____

4. Cory arrives at 5 minutes before 10.

   _____

   Practice starts at

   Is Cory early or late?

   _____

What Would You Do?

Draw a picture of an activity you would like
to do that takes the amount of time shown.

I. About I hour

2. About I0 minutes

3. About 3 days

4. About 5 hours

City Sights

A Tour of the City

Event	Time
Bus trip around the city	9:15
Visit the museum	10:30
Buggy ride in the park	12:45
Science Center dinosaur movie	2:15
Dinner at the harbor	5:30
Go to a play	7:00

Use the chart to answer the questions.

1. The museum visit lasts 2 hours. What time does it end? Draw the clock hands.

_____

2. The play lasts for 1 hour and 30 minutes. What time does it end? Draw the clock hands.

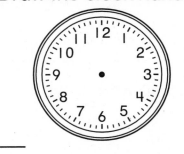

_____

3. Maggie gets to the park at 12:00. How long does she wait to take the buggy ride?

_____

4. Vinnie leaves his house at 1:15. How much time does he have to get to the Science Center before the dinosaur movie begins?

_____

Name _____

A.M. or P.M. ?

You are spending the summer at the beach.
Decide what time you will do each activity.
Write A.M. or P.M. next to each time.

Play Frisbee with the dog. _____

Have a cookout. _____

Watch the sunset. _____

Build a sandcastle. _____

Roast marshmallows. _____

Go swimming. _____

Eat breakfast. _____

Tell ghost stories. _____

Collect seashells. _____

Watch the sunrise. _____

Sing songs around
the campfire. _____

Go fishing. _____

Name _____

It's a Date

		January				
S	M	T	W	T	F	S
1	2	3	4	5	6	7
8	9	10	11	12	13	14
15	16	17	18	19	20	21
22	23	24	25	26	27	28
29	30	31				

		February				
S	M	T	W	T	F	S
			1	2	3	4
5	6	7	8	9	10	11
12	13	14	15	16	17	18
19	20	21	22	23	24	25
26	27	28				

		March				
S	M	T	W	T	F	S
			1	2	3	4
5	6	7	8	9	10	11
12	13	14	15	16	17	18
19	20	21	22	23	24	25
26	27	28	29	30	31	

Use the calendars to answer each question.

1. It is February 26th. Juan has a game on March 5th. How many more days until Juan's game?

_____ days

2. Trish went to a party on January 28th. It is February 7th. How many days have passed since the party?

_____ days

3. It is February 17th. In 14 days, Tonya has a piano recital. What is the date of Tonya's recital?

_____

4. Bill went ice skating on January 30th. One week later, the ice melted. What was the date the ice melted?

_____

Family Day

Use the schedule to answer the questions.

Family Day

Events	Starts	Ends
Sack races	1:00	2:00
Relay races	2:00	2:30
Swimming races	2:30	3:30
Arts and Crafts Show	2:00	3:30
Science Show	1:00	2:00

1. Which races last for exactly one hour each?

   _____

2. How long does the Arts and Crafts Show last?

   _____

3. How many events last exactly 60 minutes? _____

4. Which event lasts the longest?

   _____

5. Which event lasts exactly one half hour? _____

All About Shapes

Ask some classmates to choose
their favorite shape below.

Draw each shape they choose.

Make a table. Use tally marks to show
how many of each shape.

1. Which shape do children
   like the most?

   _____

2. How many children chose
   the triangle as their favorite
   shape?

   _____

3. Which shape do children
   like the least?

   _____

4. Do more children like
   circles or squares?

   _____

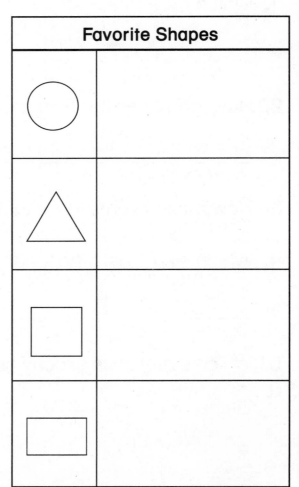

Name _____

Favorite Colors

Here is a survey that was taken in Grades 1 and 2.
Use this survey to answer the questions.

Our Favorite Colors

Color	Grade 1	Grade 2
Red	ЖТ ////	ЖТ /
Blue	ЖТ ///	////
Green	//	ЖТ //
Yellow	ЖТ	///
Pink	ЖТ /	////
Purple	///	///

1. Which color did more children choose as
   their favorite? _____

2. Do more children like green or yellow? _____

3. How many children like pink the best? _____ children

4. Do more children like blue in Grade 1
   or Grade 2? _____

5. Which color does the same number of
   children like in both grades? _____

Name _____

Cubes, Cylinders, or Cones?

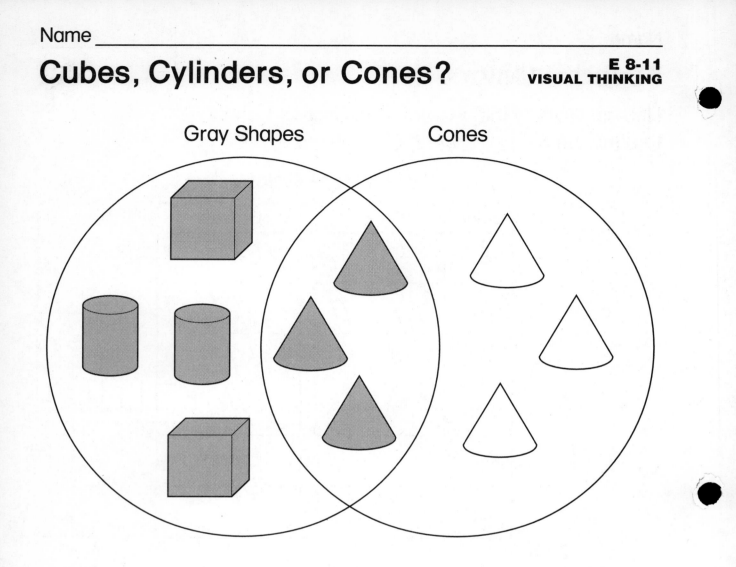

Gray Shapes   Cones

Use the Venn Diagram to answer the questions.

1. How many gray shapes are there? _____

2. How many cones are there? _____

3. How many gray cones are there? _____

4. How many shapes are gray but not cones? _____

5. How many shapes are cones but not gray? _____

At the Book Store

Use the key and the pictograph to answer
the questions.

Books Sold Last Week

Cartoon Books	📖 📖 📖 📖
Coloring Books	📖 📖 📖 📖 📖 📖 📖
Picture Books	📖 📖 📖
Animal Books	📖 📖 📖 📖 📖 📖 📖 📖 📖 📖

Each 📖 = 5 books sold

1. Which kind of book was sold the most? _____

2. How many coloring books were sold? _____

3. How many animal books were sold? _____

4. How many more animal books than
   coloring books were sold? _____

5. 5 more picture books are sold.
   How many more book symbols
   would you draw on the graph? _____

e School Play

The table shows how many tickets
the children sold for the school play.

Tickets Sold

Name	Number of Tickets
Ken	70
Lisa	30
Paul	90
Yuki	50

Make a bar graph. Color one box
for each 10 tickets sold.

Tickets Sold

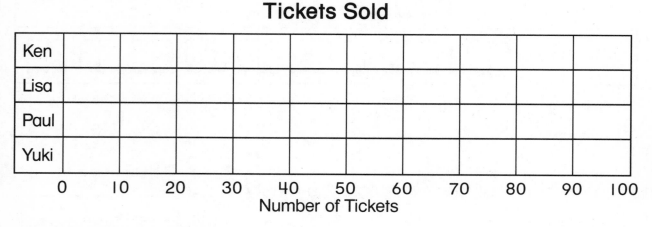

Use the bar graph and mental math
to answer each question.

1. Who sold the greatest number of tickets? _____

2. How many more tickets did Paul sell than Lisa? _____

3. Who sold fewer tickets, Lisa or Yuki? _____

   How many fewer? _____

4. How many tickets did Yuki and Lisa sell in all? _____

5. How many more tickets did Ken sell than Yuki? _____

How Many Did We Read?

Ask 10 children how many books they have read in the 2nd Grade. Record each answer on the line plot.

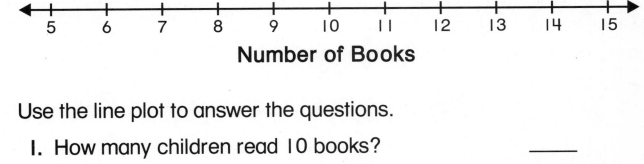

Number of Books

Use the line plot to answer the questions.

1. How many children read 10 books? _____

2. How many children read more than 10 books? _____

3. How many children read fewer than 7 books? _____

4. What is the most number of books a child read? _____

5. What is the least number of books a child read? _____

Where Will You Draw the Shapes?

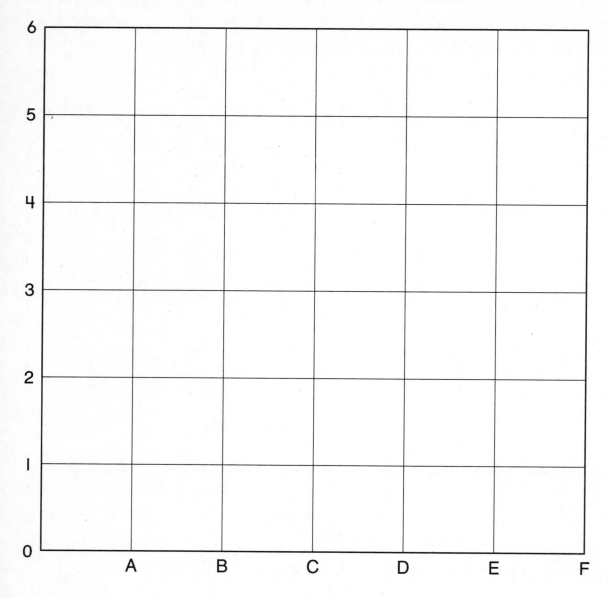

Look at the ordered pairs below.
Then draw the shapes on the graph.

1. Draw a triangle on (D, 3).	**2.** Draw a square on (A, 5).
3. Draw a circle on (E, 1).	**4.** Draw a rectangle on (B, 2).
5. Draw a triangle on (C, 4).	**6.** Draw a circle on (F, 6).

At the Amusement Park

Tickets at the amusement park come
in books of 10. The graph shows how
many books of tickets each child has.

Tickets We Have

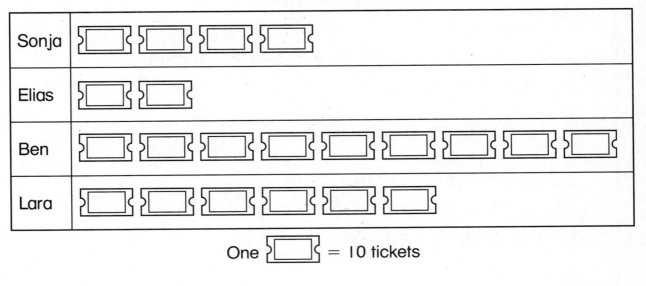

One ⊏▭⊐ = 10 tickets

1. Who has the most tickets? _____

2. How many more tickets does Ben
   have than Lara? _____

3. How many tickets do Elias and Sonja
   have in all? _____

4. The roller coaster costs 50 tickets.
   Who can ride on the roller coaster? _____

5. Write your own story problem about the graph.
   Give it to a classmate to solve.

_____

_____

All About Butterflies

Circle the time that is the most reasonable.

1. Jane colored a picture of a butterfly.
About how long did it take her?

I minute   10 minutes   100 minutes

2. Malik spent the afternoon going butterfly watching.
About how long was he watching for butterflies?

3 hours   I hour   30 hours

3. A butterfly takes about one month
to complete its growth. About how
long does it take the butterfly to grow?

I week   4 weeks   10 weeks

4. A caterpillar stays in its pupa for a couple of weeks.
About how long does the caterpillar stay in the pupa?

I day   50 days   14 days

5. Leon made a paper model of a butterfly.
About how long did it take him?

2 hours   10 hours   20 hours

Hands Up!

You can use your hand to measure.

Use your hand to measure the objects below.

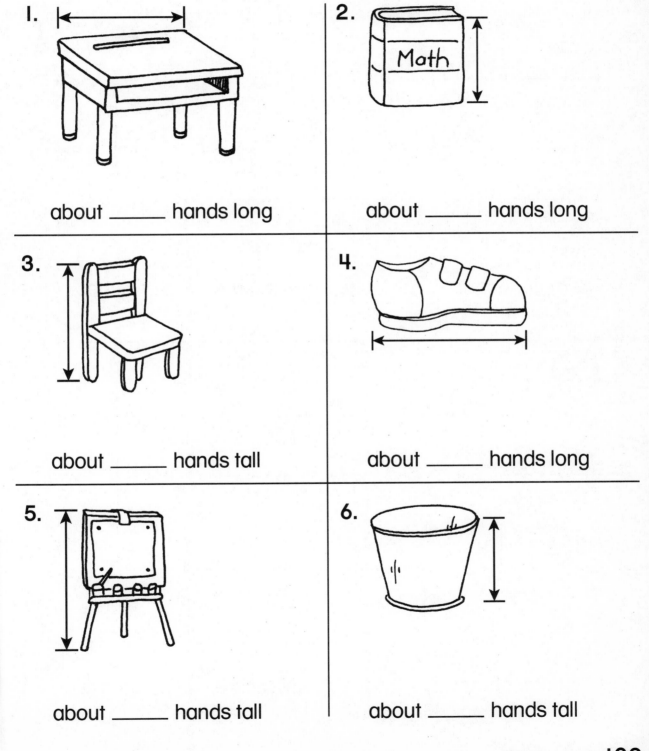

1. about _____ hands long

2. about _____ hands long

3. about _____ hands tall

4. about _____ hands long

5. about _____ hands tall

6. about _____ hands tall

Pathways Through the Park

Estimate the length of each path through the park.
Then use your inch ruler to measure.

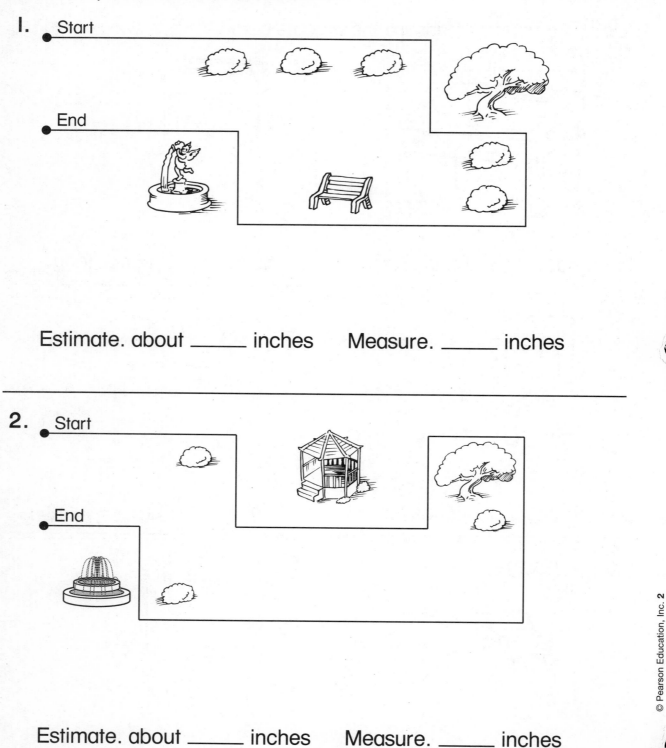

1. Start

End

Estimate. about _____ inches   Measure. _____ inches

2. Start

End

Estimate. about _____ inches   Measure. _____ inches

Name _____

What's the Measure?

Find three objects and measure their length or height.
Draw a picture or write the name of each object.
Then measure one using inches, one using feet, and
one using yards.

1.

about _____ inches

_____

2.

about _____ feet

_____

3.

about _____ yards

Race to the Cheese

Help the mice get to the cheese. Use a centimeter
ruler to draw straight lines through each maze.
Record the lengths. Then answer the questions.

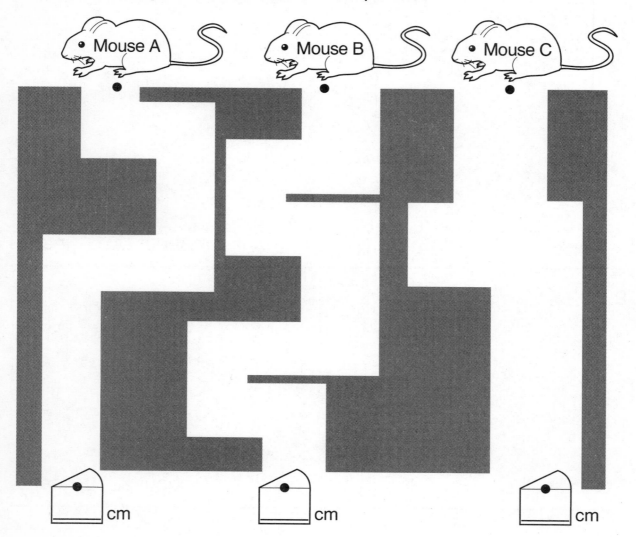

Mouse A   Mouse B   Mouse C

cm   cm   cm

1. Which mouse had the longest path to the cheese?

_____

2. Which mouse had the shortest path to the cheese?

_____

Name _____

In and Around the Shapes

E 9-5
VISUAL THINKING

Find the perimeter and area of each shape.

1.

Perimeter: _____ cm

Area: _____ square units

2.

Perimeter: _____ cm

Area: _____ square units

3.

Perimeter: _____ cm

Area: _____ square units

4.

Perimeter: _____ cm

Area: _____ square units

5. Color the shape with the longest perimeter red.

6. Color the shape with the smallest area blue.

© Pearson Education, Inc. 2

Use with Lesson 9-5. **113**

Double Measures

Circle the two containers that hold about the same amount.

1.

2.

3.

4.

5.

Cooking with Cups

| 2 cups = 1 pint |
| 4 cups = 2 pints = 1 quart |

Use the table above to rewrite the recipes.

1. Rewrite the recipe using only cups.

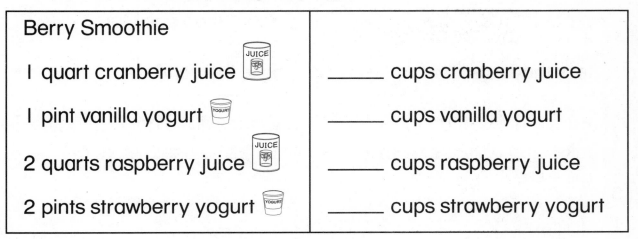

Berry Smoothie

1 quart cranberry juice   _____ cups cranberry juice

1 pint vanilla yogurt   _____ cups vanilla yogurt

2 quarts raspberry juice   _____ cups raspberry juice

2 pints strawberry yogurt   _____ cups strawberry yogurt

2. Rewrite the recipe using only pints.

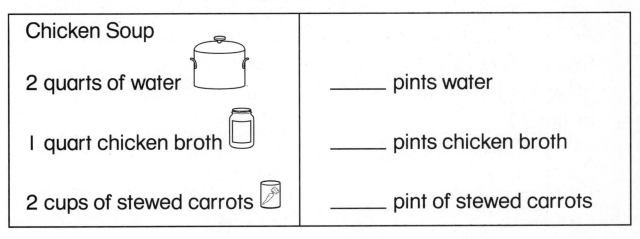

Chicken Soup

2 quarts of water   _____ pints water

1 quart chicken broth   _____ pints chicken broth

2 cups of stewed carrots   _____ pint of stewed carrots

How Much Do You Use?

Circle the most reasonable answer.

1. Liza makes a pitcher of lemonade for her family. Does she use more or less than one liter of water?

   more than one liter

   less than one liter

2. Maria makes a cup of tea for her friend. Does she use more or less than one liter of water?

   more than one liter

   less than one liter

3. Edmund fills a tub to take a bath. Does he use 40 liters or 4 liters?

   40 liters

   4 liters

4. Carlos fills a goldfish bowl. Does he use 3 liters or 30 liters?

   3 liters

   30 liters

5. Ari helps clean the classroom tables. Does he use 1 liter of water or 10 liters of water?

   1 liter

   10 liters

6. Bonnie fills a washtub to wash her dog. Does she use 5 liters or 25 liters of water?

   5 liters

   25 liters

Finding Cubic Units

Use the data in the chart to fill each box with cubes.
Then complete the chart.

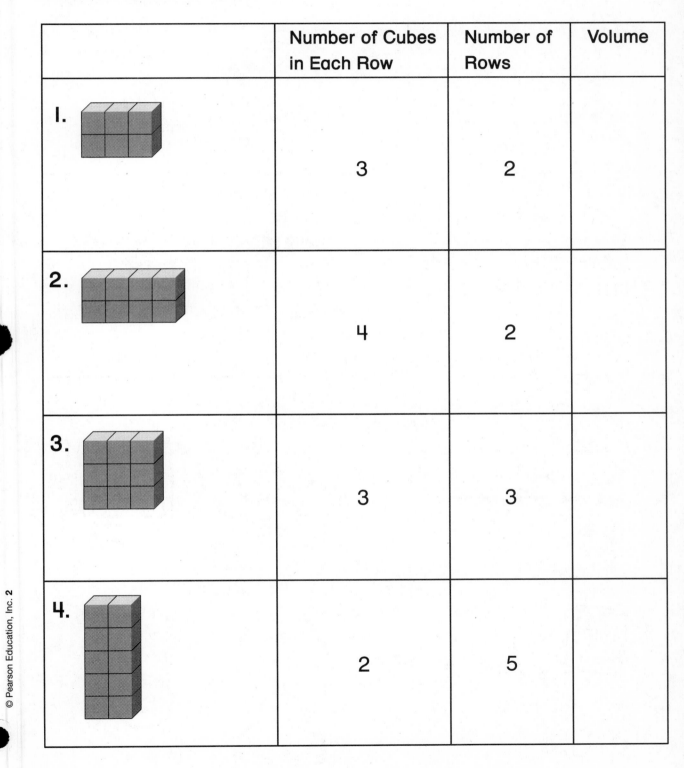

	Number of Cubes in Each Row	Number of Rows	Volume
1.	3	2	
2.	4	2	
3.	3	3	
4.	2	5	

Name _____

A Balancing Act

Circle the object that would make the scale balance.

1.

2.

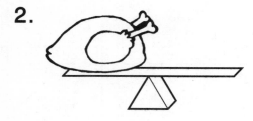 

3.

4.

Name _____

Pounds or Ounces?

Circle the most reasonable answer.

1. Dana makes a peanut butter sandwich. Does she use 1 ounce or 1 pound of peanut butter?

   1 ounce

   1 pound

2. Enrico makes a glass of fruit drink. Does he use 5 ounces or 5 pounds of fruit for the drink?

   5 ounces

   5 pounds

3. Eric buys apples to make an apple pie. Does he get 3 ounces or 3 pounds of apples?

   3 ounces

   3 pounds

4. Steven makes hamburgers for a party. Does each hamburger weigh 4 ounces or 4 pounds?

   4 ounces

   4 pounds

5. Sonya makes a pizza with cheese. Does she use 10 ounces or 10 pounds of cheese?

   10 ounces

   10 pounds

6. Megan wants to weigh her baby kitten. Does the kitten weigh 16 ounces or 16 pounds?

   16 ounces

   16 pounds

© Pearson Education, Inc. 2

Animal Measures

Does each animal measure less than 1 kilogram, about
1 kilogram, or more than 1 kilogram? Write the name
of the animal in the chart under its measure. Then think
of another animal you can add to each measure.

frog   pig   turtle   goldfish

guinea pig   seal   mouse   kitten   wolf

Less than 1 kilogram	About 1 kilogram	More than 1 kilogram
_____	_____	_____
_____	_____	_____
_____	_____	_____
My choice:	My choice:	My choice:

Let's Play Outdoors

Draw a picture of the clothes you might
wear outdoors for each temperature.

I. 85°F

2. 25°F

3. 25°C

4. 5°C

Spinner Fun

Pick 2 colors. Color the spinner. You must use 1 color more than once. Then answer the questions.

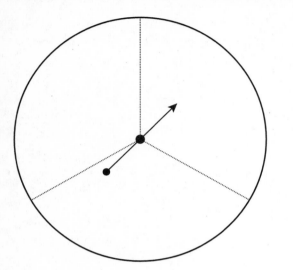

Tell which colors the spinner is least likely and most likely to land on.

1. least likely _____

2. most likely _____

Color 1 section of the spinner yellow. Color 2 sections of the spinner blue. Color 3 sections of the spinner red. Then answer the questions.

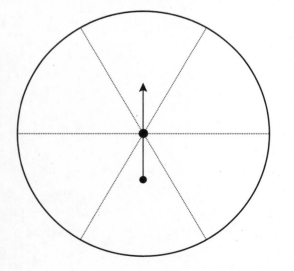

Tell which colors the spinner is least likely and most likely to land on.

3. least likely _____

4. most likely _____

Mostly Marbles

Count the number of marbles in each bag. Use tally marks.
Then circle the missing word to complete the sentence.

White Marbles	Black Marbles

1. You pick 4 marbles out of the bag.
It is _____ that you will
pick a white marble.

　　　impossible　　　　possible　　　　certain

White Marbles	Black Marbles

2. You pick 10 marbles out of the bag.
It is _____ that you will
pick some black marbles.

　　　impossible　　　　possible　　　　certain

Try the exercises above using red and blue cubes.
Do your results match? Write about what you found.

_____

_____

Name _____

At the Farm

Mr. and Mrs. Morley picked their crops. Use the data
in the chart to answer each question.

Number of Pounds Picked

Apples	Peaches	Pumpkins	Corn	Squash
35	23	47	25	17

1. Mr. Morley took the apples and
   the peaches to the fruit stand.
   How many pounds of fruit
   did he take?   _____ pounds

   Then he sold 13 pounds of
   peaches. How many pounds
   of fruit does he have at
   the fruit stand now?   _____ pounds

2. Mrs. Morley took the corn and
   the squash to the vegetable stand.
   How many pounds of vegetables
   did she take?   _____ pounds

   Then she took all the pumpkins
   to the stand. How many pounds
   of vegetables does she have
   at the stand now?   _____ pounds

3. Write your own two-step problem. Use the data in the chart.

   _____

   _____

Choose the Unit

Choose the best estimate of measure for each object.

1. Tracy wants to measure a ribbon to use as a necklace.

   About 2 centimeters

   About 40 centimeters

   About 500 centimeters

2. Jerome wants to measure some apples for a pie.

   About 3 pounds

   About 15 pounds

   About 25 pounds

3. Doreen measures fruit juice for her classroom party.

   About 1 liter

   About 3 liters

   About 75 liters

4. Roberto measures some fabric for a tablecloth.

   About 2 yards

   About 17 yards

   About 35 yards

5. Opal measures a board to cut for the roof of a birdhouse.

   About 2 inches

   About 83 inches

   About 8 inches

6. Jamal measures the length of a full basketball court.

   About 7 feet

   About 18 feet

   About 94 feet

Name _____

A Secret Treasure

Help the children find the treasure.

Count by 100s to find the 1,000 gold coins.

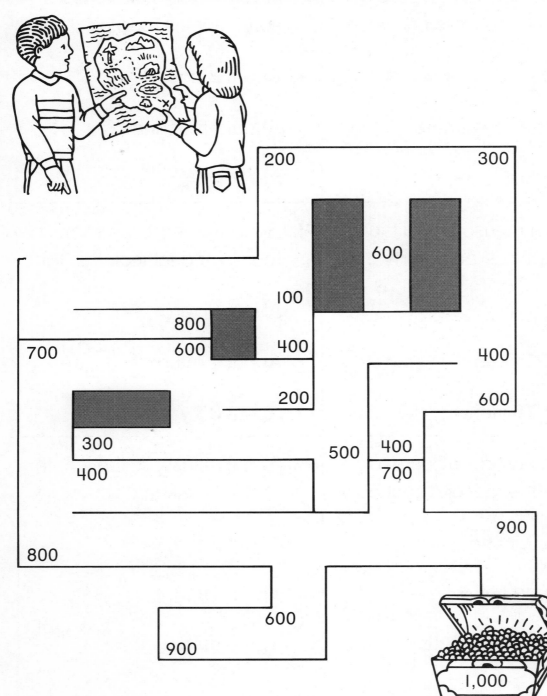

Mail Match

Use the jumbled clues to find each person's mailbox.
Then draw a line from each person to the correct mailbox.

Clues   **Mailboxes**

1. My mailbox has 1 hundred,
   8 ones, and 9 tens.

   It is _____.

   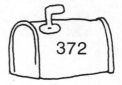
   372

2. My mailbox has 1 ten,
   7 hundreds, and 4 ones.

   It is _____.

   506

3. My mailbox has 3 hundreds,
   2 ones, and 7 tens.

   It is _____.

   198

4. My mailbox has 3 tens,
   5 ones, and 6 hundreds.

   It is _____.

   714

5. My mailbox has 6 ones,
   5 hundreds, and 0 tens.

   It is _____.

   635

A Number Crossword

Use the clues to fill in the number puzzle.

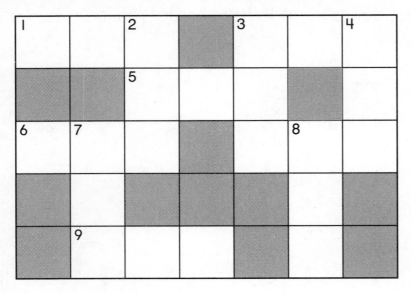

Across

1. 500 + 20 + 3

3.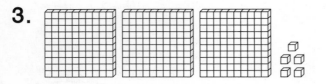

5. 400 + 20 + 9

6.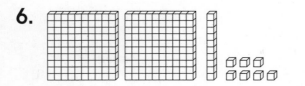

9. Two hundred sixty-nine

Down

2. 300 + 40 + 7

3. Three hundred ninety-seven

4. 500 + 60 + 9

7.

8. Four hundred thirty-eight

Trick Hats

What number is hidden inside the hat?
Use mental math to solve. Write the missing number.

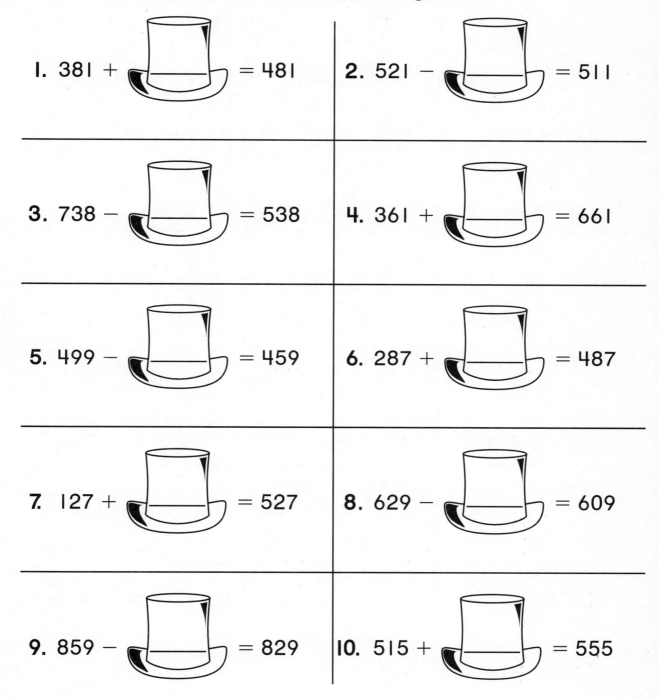

1. 381 + ⬜ = 481

2. 521 − ⬜ = 511

3. 738 − ⬜ = 538

4. 361 + ⬜ = 661

5. 499 − ⬜ = 459

6. 287 + ⬜ = 487

7. 127 + ⬜ = 527

8. 629 − ⬜ = 609

9. 859 − ⬜ = 829

10. 515 + ⬜ = 555

Number Triangles

Use the numbers in the triangles.
Write a number that will make each sentence true.

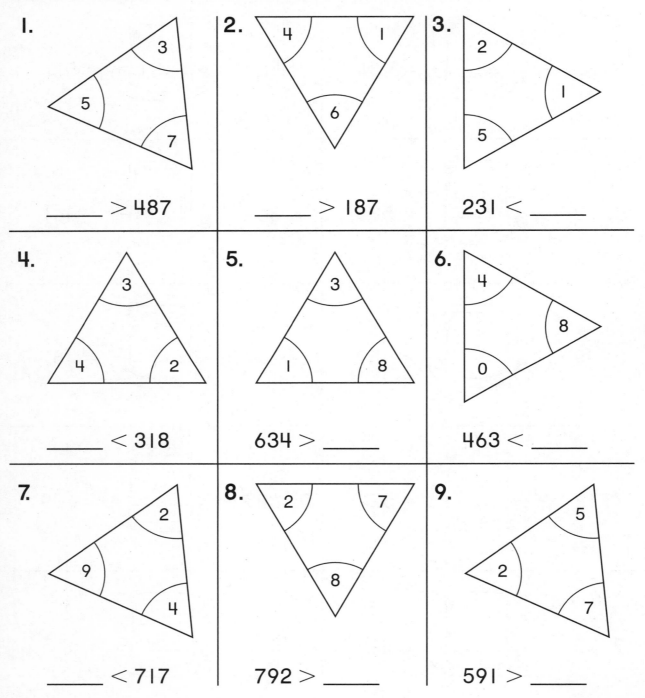

1.

_____ > 487

2.

_____ > 187

3.

231 < _____

4.

_____ < 318

5.

634 > _____

6.

463 < _____

7.

_____ < 717

8.

792 > _____

9.

591 > _____

Bean Bag Toss

Four children play bean bag toss.

They already have some points.

Color the 2 numbers they must hit to make 1,000.

Then complete each number sentence.

1. Vanessa has 300 points.

200	500
600	300

300 + _____ + _____ = 1,000

2. Leroy has 250 points.

150	250
600	550

250 + _____ + _____ = 1,000

3. Maya has 450 points.

450	300
150	400

450 + _____ + _____ = 1,000

4. Chin has 200 points.

200	550
250	400

200 + _____ + _____ = 1,000

Name _____

At the Movies

Choose five different numbers that have 3 digits.
Write the numbers in the chart.
Then use the numbers to answer the questions.

Movie Tickets Sold

Monday	Tuesday	Wednesday	Thursday	Friday
_____	_____	_____	_____	_____

1. Were more tickets sold on
   Wednesday or Thursday?   _____

2. How many tickets were sold
   on Monday?   _____

3. On what day were the most
   tickets sold?   _____

4. Were more tickets sold on
   Thursday or Friday?   _____

5. Write the expanded number
   for the number of tickets sold
   on Tuesday.   _____ + _____ + _____

6. Write your own problem. Have a friend solve it.

_____

_____

Team Shirts

Five players came to play soccer.
Look at the clues and the numbers in the box.
Match the players with their team number.
Write the number on the shirt.

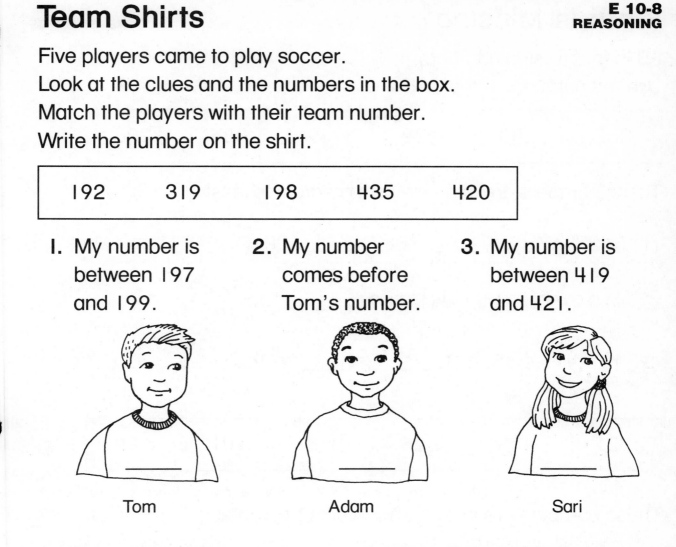

| 192 | 319 | 198 | 435 | 420 |

1. My number is between 197 and 199.

Tom

2. My number comes before Tom's number.

Adam

3. My number is between 419 and 421.

Sari

4. My number comes after Sari's number.

Ming

5. My number is between Tom's and Sari's number.

Carlos

What Is Missing?

Fill in the missing numbers.
Use the numbers in the box.

| 362 | 240 | 429 | 719 | 885 | 226 |

These numbers are in order from greatest to least.

1. 562, 467, 431, _____, 387, _____, 341

2. 973, 960, _____, 841, 769, _____, 700

3. 437, 411, 365, 271, _____, _____, 199

| 321 | 478 | 625 | 415 | 701 | 589 |

These numbers are in order from least to greatest.

4. 215, 297, _____, 341, 402, _____, 437

5. 482, 521, 618, _____, _____, 750

6. 389, 413, 459, _____, 532, _____, 599

Name _____

Pattern Addition and Subtraction

Write the number in the pattern.

Then describe the pattern rule.

Then write the next number in the pattern.

I. $203 +$? $= 223,\ 223 +$? $= 243,\ 243 +$? $= 263$

The numbers (increase) / decrease by 20. The next number is 283.

2. $530 -$? $= 430,\ 430 -$? $= 330,\ 330 -$? $= 230$

The numbers increase / decrease by _____. The next number is _____.

3. $720 +$? $= 730,\ 730 +$? $= 740,\ 740 +$? $= 750$

The numbers increase / decrease by _____. The next number is _____.

4. $305 +$? $= 405,\ 405 +$? $= 505,\ 505 +$? $= 605$

The numbers increase / decrease by _____. The next number is _____.

5. $852 -$? $= 752,\ 752 -$? $= 652,\ 652 -$? $= 552$

The numbers increase / decrease by _____. The next number is _____.

6. $785 -$? $= 765,\ 765 -$? $= 745,\ 745 -$? $= 725$

The numbers increase / decrease by _____. The next number is _____.

Let's Roll!

The table shows how many miles these rescue vehicles drove in one month. Use the data in the chart to answer each question.

Rescue Vehicles	
Fire Engine 1	386
Fire Engine 2	571
Ambulance	489
Fireboat	214

1. The ambulance rides another 100 miles.
   How many miles is that in all?   _____ miles

2. What is the number of hundreds, tens,
   and ones that the fireboat drove?   _____ hundreds

                                                     _____ tens

                                                     _____ ones

3. Compare the number of miles driven
   by Fire Engine 1 and Fire Engine 2.

   Write >, <, or =.   386 ◯ 571

4. Fire Engine 3 drove 10 miles
   less than Fire Engine 1.
   How many miles did it drive?   _____ miles

5. Write your own problem about the numbers in the chart.
   Give your problem to a classmate to solve.

   _____

   _____

   _____

Missing Numbers

Use mental math to find the missing digit
of each number. Then write the number.

1. $236 + 1\square2 = 378$

_____

2. $314 + \square23 = 537$

_____

3. $524 + 15\square = 675$

_____

4. $3\square2 + 442 = 794$

_____

5. $\square35 + 402 = 837$

_____

6. $\square48 + 140 = 888$

_____

7. $15\square + 126 = 279$

_____

8. $251 + \square35 = 486$

_____

9. $305 + 3\square2 = 607$

_____

10. $\square21 + 344 = 565$

_____

The Raffle

Use the data in the table to record how many
tickets each child sold. Then estimate the sums
to answer the questions.

Raffle Tickets Sold

Marissa	Benji	Amita	Steven	Nicky
127	415	378	292	134

1. Amita sold _____ tickets.

   Steven sold _____ tickets.

   Did they sell more than
   600 tickets together?

   yes   no

2. Marissa sold _____ tickets.

   Nicky sold _____ tickets.

   Did they sell more than
   400 tickets together?

   yes   no

3. Benji sold _____ tickets.

   Marissa sold _____ tickets.

   Did they sell more than
   500 tickets together?

   yes   no

4. Amita sold _____ tickets.

   Benji sold _____ tickets.

   Did they sell more than
   700 tickets together?

   yes   no

5. Nicky sold _____ tickets.

   Benji sold _____ tickets.

   Did they sell less than
   500 tickets together?

   yes   no

6. Steven sold _____ tickets.

   Marissa sold _____ tickets.

   Did they sell less than
   400 tickets together?

   yes   no

Around the Playground

Use the map and models to find the sums.

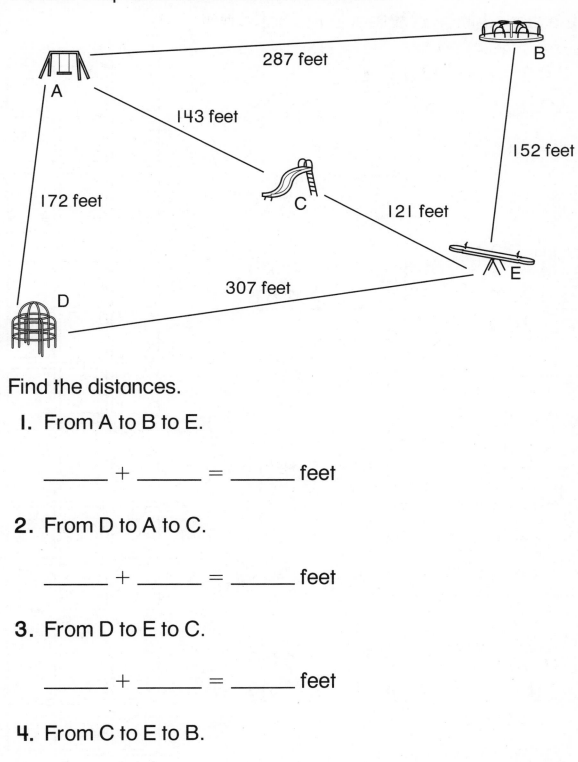

287 feet

143 feet

B

152 feet

A

172 feet

C

121 feet

E

D

307 feet

Find the distances.

1. From A to B to E.

_____ + _____ = _____ feet

2. From D to A to C.

_____ + _____ = _____ feet

3. From D to E to C.

_____ + _____ = _____ feet

4. From C to E to B.

_____ + _____ = _____ feet

Add Over Again

Add. Look for the pattern.
Write the last addition problem in the pattern.

1. $\begin{array}{r} 209 \\ +123 \end{array}$ $\begin{array}{r} 309 \\ +223 \end{array}$ $\begin{array}{r} 409 \\ +323 \end{array}$

2. $\begin{array}{r} 134 \\ +252 \end{array}$ $\begin{array}{r} 154 \\ +254 \end{array}$ $\begin{array}{r} 174 \\ +256 \end{array}$

3. $\begin{array}{r} 315 \\ +427 \end{array}$ $\begin{array}{r} 415 \\ +327 \end{array}$ $\begin{array}{r} 515 \\ +227 \end{array}$

4. $\begin{array}{r} 570 \\ +118 \end{array}$ $\begin{array}{r} 560 \\ +218 \end{array}$ $\begin{array}{r} 550 \\ +318 \end{array}$

Going Up

This elevator holds up to 300 pounds.

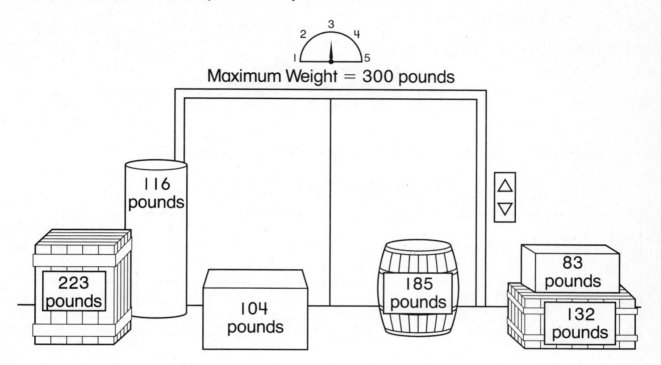

Maximum Weight = 300 pounds

All of these containers need to get to the top floor.
What combinations of two containers can ride in the
elevator? Write some addition problems to find out.
You may use the same container more than one time.

Trip 1	Trip 2	Trip 3

Name _____

Come Fly with Me!

Sam, Josh, and Mary
are pilots. Use the chart
to answer the questions.

Number of Miles Flown

	Friday	Saturday	Sunday
Sam	350	250	100
Josh	100	150	100
Mary	400	100	50

1. Use the data from the chart to complete the graph.

Number of Miles Flown

Sam															
Josh															
Mary															

0 50 100 150 200 250 300 350 400 450 500 550 600 650 700 750

2. The next Monday, Josh flew 150 miles.
   He flew 200 miles on Tuesday.
   How many miles did he fly on those two days? _____

   Add the new information to the graph.

3. Mary flies 200 more miles. Use the graph
   to show how many miles Mary flew in all.

4. Write a problem using the information in the graph.
   Give your problem to a classmate to solve.

_____

_____

_____

The Craft Store

Use the pictures to answer the questions.
Count on or count back to solve.

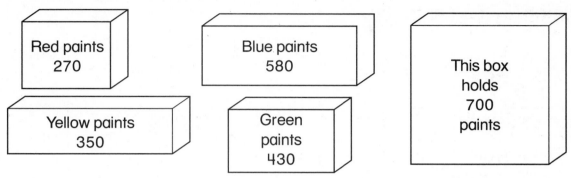

Red paints
270

Blue paints
580

Yellow paints
350

Green
paints
430

This box
holds
700
paints

1. Ms. Hoople wants to pack the
   yellow paints in the big box.
   How many more paints will
   the big box hold?   _____

2. Mr. Bromley wants to pack the
   blue paints in the big box.
   How many more paints will
   the big box hold?   _____

3. Which two boxes will fit exactly into the big box?
   Write an addition problem to show your answer.

   _____

   _____

4. Ms. Hoople puts the yellow paints in the big box.
   What other box will fit? Explain.

   _____

   _____

Puzzle Boxes

Estimate down or across the boxes.
Color the outside boxes that match
the estimate in the center box.

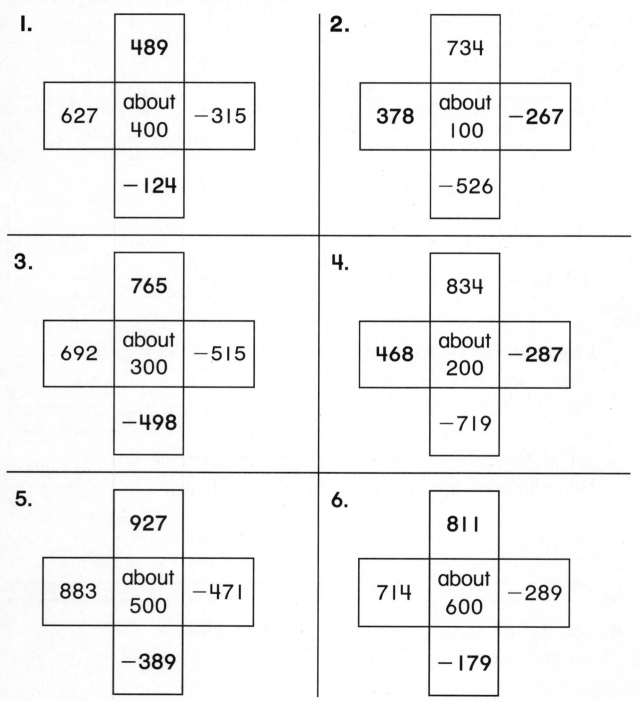

1.

489

627 | about 400 | −315

−124

2.

734

378 | about 100 | −267

−526

3.

765

692 | about 300 | −515

−498

4.

834

468 | about 200 | −287

−719

5.

927

883 | about 500 | −471

−389

6.

811

714 | about 600 | −289

−179

The Toy Store

Use the data in the chart to help Mr. Mickle find out
how many toys were sold. Use models and Workmat 5
to help you subtract. Then answer the questions below.

Toys	Started With	Left	Sold
Train Sets	532	215	
Dolls	674	429	
Games	427	119	
Puzzles	387	215	
Building Blocks	259	163	

1. Which toy sold the most? _____

2. Which toy sold the least? _____

3. How many more games than puzzles were sold?
Use models to subtract. _____

Tic-Tac Subtract

I. Subtract to find the differences.

Hundreds	Tens	Ones
4	3	7
− 1	6	4

Hundreds	Tens	Ones
5	7	8
− 2	6	4

Hundreds	Tens	Ones
6	2	3
− 3	7	1

Hundreds	Tens	Ones
9	1	7
− 2	3	2

354

Hundreds	Tens	Ones
7	5	3
− 2	4	9

Hundreds	Tens	Ones
3	8	1
− 1	9	0

Hundreds	Tens	Ones
8	4	3
− 4	2	8

Hundreds	Tens	Ones
9	8	9
− 3	6	2

2. Look at the differences in each problem above.
Find two that you can subtract to make a difference
of 354. Draw a line to connect the problems.

Teamwork

Choose one player from each team. Write
a subtraction problem using their scores.
Then write how many more points the player
from the A Team scored.

A Team Score

Marco	745
Elena	916
Dekembi	692
Linda	885

B Team Score

Jackie	452
Kalisha	325
Dante	581
Akmad	263

Subtraction Problems

I. A Team Player _____

   B Team Player _____

   A Team scored _____ more points.

2. A Team Player _____

   B Team Player _____

   A Team scored _____ more points.

3. A Team Player _____

   B Team Player _____

   A Team scored _____ more points.

Name ______________________________

The Play's the Thing

E 11-12
REASONING

The chart shows how many people came to the school play on each day.

People at the School Play	
Thursday	135
Friday	213
Saturday	167
Sunday	152

1. Use the information in the chart to write a problem that has an exact answer. Solve the problem.

____

____

____

____

____

2. Use the information in the chart to write a problem that can be answered with an estimate. Solve the problem.

____

____

____

____

____

Rain Forest Animals

Circle the most reasonable answer.

1. A toucan flies 250 yards. Then it flies some more. About how many yards does the toucan fly?

about 350 yards

about 250 yards

about 150 feet

2. A mother tree sloth climbs 560 feet. A baby tree sloth climbs less than the mother. About how many feet does the baby tree sloth climb?

about 560 feet

about 560 yards

about 400 feet

3. A monkey climbs 90 feet up a tree. Then the monkey climbs a little farther. About how high is the monkey?

about 125 feet

about 20 yards

about 500 inches

4. A big tree is 235 feet tall. A smaller tree is next to the big tree. About how tall is the shorter tree?

about 150 feet

about 100 yards

about 300 feet

5. A python snake is 396 inches long. An anaconda snake is 267 inches long. How much longer is the python snake?

_____ inches

Puppies and Kittens

Look at the pictures. Write how many in all.

1. How many legs?

_____ groups of _____ legs

_____ legs in all

2. How many spots?

_____ groups of _____ spots

_____ spots in all

3. How many tails?

_____ groups of _____ tail

_____ tails in all

4. How many stripes?

_____ groups of _____ stripes

_____ stripes in all

5. Draw a picture. Write your own problem to go with the picture.

_____

_____

Ball Toss

3 children toss balls into baskets. Write number sentences that tell how many balls are tossed in all.

1.

_____ + _____ + _____ + _____ = _____

_____ × _____ = _____

2.

_____ + _____ + _____ + _____ + _____ + _____ = _____

_____ × _____ = _____

3.

_____ + _____ + _____ = _____

_____ × _____ = _____

4. Use the clues to match the name of each child to the correct ball toss above. Write the number of tosses each child made.

Louis tosses as many balls as Rita.
Rita tosses 4 more balls than Bill.

Louis _____   Rita _____   Bill _____

Name _____

An Array of Arrays

Color an array for each product below.
Write the multiplication sentence.

1. Red: Color an array for 8 in all. _____ × _____ = 8

2. Blue: Color an array for 10 in all. _____ × _____ = 10

3. Green: Color an array for 12 in all. _____ × _____ = 12

4. Yellow: Color an array for 15 in all. _____ × _____ = 15

5. Orange: Color an array for 16 in all. _____ × _____ = 16

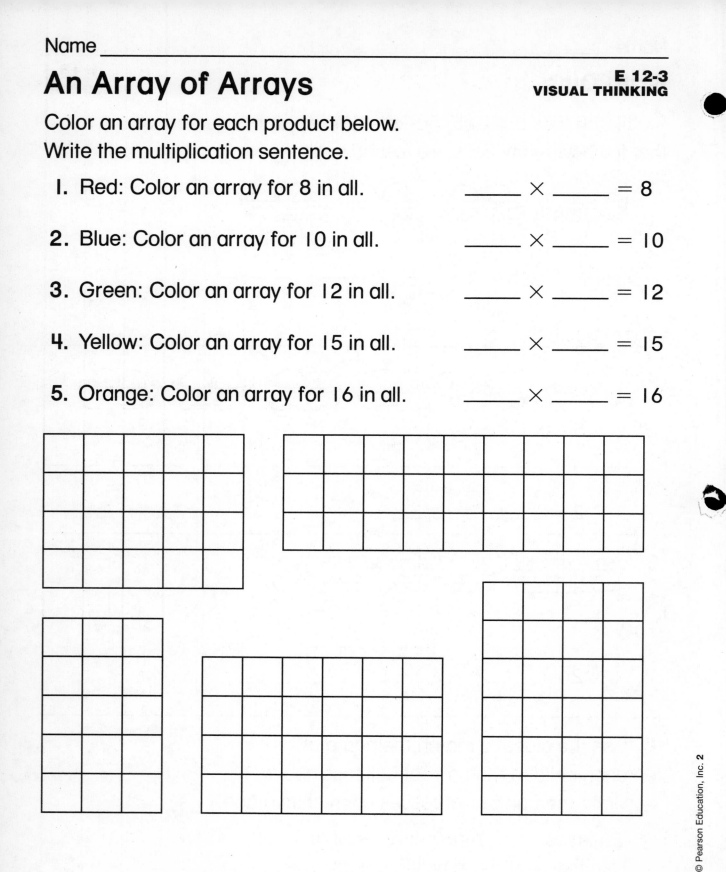

Multiplication Match

Complete each number sentence. Then draw
a line from the number sentence in Column A
to the matching number sentence in Column B.

Column A

1. $4 \times 1 =$ _____

2. $3 \times 6 =$ _____

3. $2 \times 5 =$ _____

4. $7 \times 2 =$ _____

5. $6 \times 2 =$ _____

6. $4 \times 2 =$ _____

7. $3 \times 5 =$ _____

8. $6 \times 4 =$ _____

9. $1 \times 7 =$ _____

Column B

$5 \times 2 =$ _____

$2 \times 4 =$ _____

$1 \times 4 =$ _____

$6 \times 3 =$ _____

$5 \times 3 =$ _____

$2 \times 7 =$ _____

$2 \times 6 =$ _____

$7 \times 1 =$ _____

$4 \times 6 =$ _____

At the Bakery

Multiply. Then draw lines to match
each picture with 2 different multiplication facts.

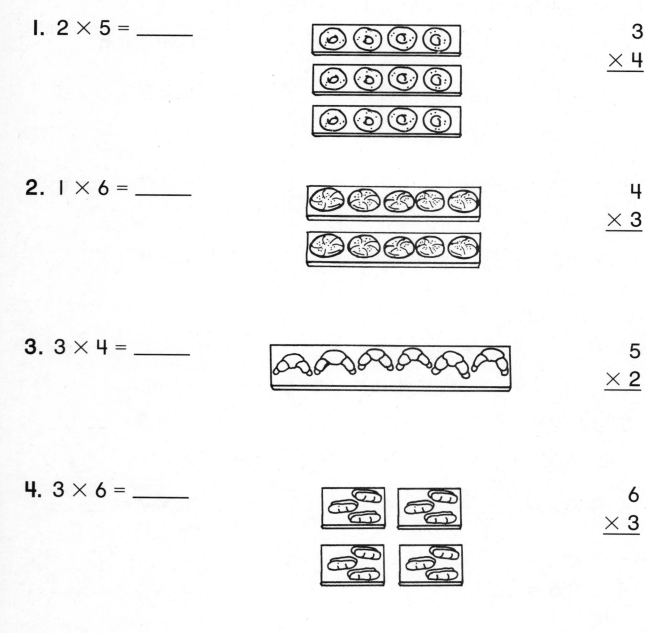

1. $2 \times 5 =$ _____

3
$\times 4$

2. $1 \times 6 =$ _____

4
$\times 3$

3. $3 \times 4 =$ _____

5
$\times 2$

4. $3 \times 6 =$ _____

6
$\times 3$

5. $4 \times 3 =$ _____

6
$\times 1$

At the Hobby Store

Draw 4 window displays for Mr. Morgan's Hobby Store.
Choose a group of items to draw in each window.
Write a multiplication sentence for each.

balls: 4 rows, 3 balls in each	crayon boxes: 3 rows, 3 crayon boxes in each	paint jars: 4 rows, 4 paint jars in each
blocks: 5 rows, 3 blocks in each	rolls of ribbon: 2 rows, 3 rolls of ribbon in each	spools of thread: 2 rows, 4 spools of thread in each

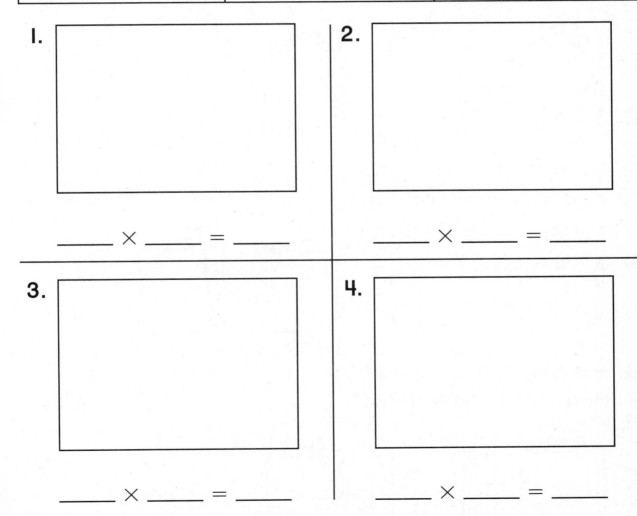

1.

_____ × _____ = _____

2.

_____ × _____ = _____

3.

_____ × _____ = _____

4.

_____ × _____ = _____

Party Time

Sue is putting these toys into bags. She wants
to make equal shares. Draw the equal shares.
Write how many toys go in each bag.

1. Sue puts the jacks in 3 bags.
   How many jacks are in each bag?

   _____ jacks

2. Sue puts the tops in 4 bags.
   How many are in each bag?

   _____ tops

3. Sue puts the whistles in 3 bags.
   How many are in each bag?

   _____ whistles

At the Farmer's Market

Draw the fruit in boxes to show equal groups.
Then write a division sentence.

1. There are 12 oranges in all.

_____ ÷ _____ = _____

2. There are 8 apples in all.

_____ ÷ _____ = _____

3. There are 9 tomatoes in all.

_____ ÷ _____ = _____

4. There are 6 watermelons in all.

_____ ÷ _____ = _____

Name _____

At the Supermarket

Decide if you will add, subtract, multiply, or
divide to solve each problem. Write the number
sentence to solve the problem.

1. Charlene has 5 rows of soup cans with 4 in each row.
   How many soup cans are there?

   ☐ ○ ☐ = ☐

   _____ soup cans

2. There are 12 boxes of cereal in
   one carton. Mr. Mooney puts
   6 boxes on a shelf. How many
   cereal boxes are still in the carton?

   ☐ ○ ☐ = ☐

   _____ cereal boxes

3. Will puts an equal number of steaks in
   2 bins. There are 10 steaks in all.
   How many steaks go in each bin?

   ☐ ○ ☐ = ☐

   _____ steaks

4. There are 16 loaves of bread in a box.
   Mrs. Melon buys 4 loaves. How many
   loaves of bread are left in the box?

   ☐ ○ ☐ = ☐

   _____ loaves of bread

Name _____

Arithmetic Airport

Use mental math to solve.

1. Christy has 20 pounds of luggage.
   Martin has twice as many pounds of
   luggage as she does. How many pounds
   does Martin have?   _____ pounds

   _____

2. The waiting area has 3 rows of seats.
   There are 6 seats in each row. How many
   seats are there in all?   _____ seats

   _____

3. Glen waits in line to board the plane.
   There are 25 people in the line.
   Glen is fourth in line. How many people
   are behind him?   _____ people

   _____

4. There are 16 sandwiches and 4 trays
   at the snack bar. Ms. Marshall puts an
   equal number of sandwiches on each tray.
   How many sandwiches go on each tray?   _____ sandwiches

   _____

5. Write your own math problem about the airport.
   Give it to a friend to solve.

   _____

   _____

   _____

   _____